Safety in the installation and use of gas systems and appliances

Gas Safety (Installation and Use) Regulations 1998

Approved Code of Practice and guidance

HSE Books

© Crown copyright 2011

First published 1994
Second edition 1998
Reprinted with amendments (twice) 2000, 2001 (twice), 2002, 2004, 2007 (twice)
Third edition 2011

ISBN 978 0 7176 6419 1

You may reuse this information (not including logos) free of charge in any format or medium, under the terms of the Open Government Licence. To view the licence visit www.nationalarchives.gov.uk/doc/open-government-licence/, write to the Information Policy Team, The National Archives, Kew, London TW9 4DU, or email psi@nationalarchives.gsi.gov.uk.

Some images and illustrations may not be owned by the Crown so cannot be reproduced without permission of the copyright owner. Enquiries should be sent to copyright@hse.gsi.gov.uk.

Approved Code of Practice and guidance

This Code has been approved by the Health and Safety Commission, with the consent of the Secretary of State. It gives practical advice on how to comply with the law. If you follow the advice you will be doing enough to comply with the law in respect of those specific matters on which the Code gives advice. You may use alternative methods to those set out in the Code in order to comply with the law.

However, the Code has special legal status. If you are prosecuted for breach of health and safety law, and it is proved that you did not follow the relevant provisions of the Code, you will need to show that you have complied with the law in some other way or a court will find you at fault.

The Regulations and Approved Code of Practice are accompanied by guidance which does not form part of the ACOP. Following the guidance is not compulsory and you are free to take other action. But if you do follow the guidance you will normally be doing enough to comply with the law. Health and safety inspectors seek to secure compliance with the law and may refer to this guidance as illustrating good practice.

Contents

Notice of Approval *(v)*

Introduction *1*

Part A General *8*

Regulation 1   Citation and commencement   *8*
Regulation 2   General interpretation and application   *8*

Part B Gas fittings – general provisions *20*

Regulation 3   Qualification and supervision   *20*
Regulation 4   Duty on employer   *22*
Regulation 5   Materials and workmanship   *23*
Regulation 6   General safety precautions   *24*
Regulation 7   Protection against damage   *26*
Regulation 8   Existing gas fittings   *27*
Regulation 9   Emergency controls   *29*
Regulation 10   Maintaining electrical continuity   *31*

Part C Meters and regulators *32*

Regulation 11   Interpretation of Part C   *32*
Regulation 12   Meters – general provisions   *32*
Regulation 13   Meter housings   *33*
Regulation 14   Regulators   *34*
Regulation 15   Meters – emergency notices   *36*
Regulation 16   Primary meters   *36*
Regulation 17   Secondary meters   *38*

Part D Installation pipework *40*

Regulation 18   Safe use of pipes   *40*
Regulation 19   Enclosed pipes   *41*
Regulation 20   Protection of buildings   *42*
Regulation 21   Clogging precautions   *42*
Regulation 22   Testing and purging of pipes   *42*
Regulation 23   Marking of pipes   *44*
Regulation 24   Large consumers   *44*

Part E Gas appliances *46*

Regulation 25   Interpretation of Part E   *46*
Regulation 26   Gas appliances – safety precautions   *46*
Regulation 27   Flues   *49*
Regulation 28   Access   *50*
Regulation 29   Manufacturer's instructions   *50*
Regulation 30   Room-sealed appliances   *50*
Regulation 31   Suspended appliances   *51*
Regulation 32   Flue dampers   *52*
Regulation 33   Testing of appliances   *52*
Regulation 34   Use of appliances   *54*

Part F Maintenance *56*

Regulation 35   Duties of employers and self-employed persons   *56*
Regulation 36   Duties of landlords   *57*

Part G Miscellaneous *65*

Regulation 37 Escape of gas *65*
Regulation 38 Use of antifluctuators and valves *68*
Regulation 39 Exception as to liability *69*
Regulation 40 Exemption certificates *69*
Regulation 41 Revocation and amendments *70*

Appendix 1 Requirements for appliances and flues *71*

Appendix 2 Examples of potentially unsafe situations (regulation 34) *74*

Appendix 3 Summary of legislation *77*

Appendix 4 Appropriate standards, ACOPs, guidance and relevant information sources *82*

Appendix 5 Diagrams of typical installations *92*

Notice of Approval

By virtue of section 16(1) of the Health and Safety at Work etc Act 1974, and with the consent of the Secretary of State for the Environment, Transport and the Regions, the Health and Safety Commission has on 8 September 1998 approved a Code of Practice which provides practical guidance with respect to the provisions of the Gas Safety (Installation and Use) Regulations 1998.

The Code of Practice consists of those paragraphs which are identified as such in the document entitled Safety in the installation and use of gas systems and appliances.

The Code of Practice comes into effect on 31 October 1998.

Signed

R A BANNER
Secretary to the Health and Safety Commission

12 October 1998

The Health and Safety Commission (HSC) and the Health and Safety Executive (HSE) merged on 1 April 2008 to form a single national regulatory body. From that date, the Health and Safety Executive became responsible for approving Codes of Practice, with the consent of the Secretary of State.

Introduction

Background

This Approved Code of Practice (ACOP) and guidance gives practical advice to those with responsibilities under the Gas Safety (Installation and Use) Regulations 1998 (SI 1998 No 2451) (GSIUR). It has been drawn up in consultation with representatives of the Confederation of British Industry, the Trades Union Congress, local authorities, government departments, consumer organisations and the Health and Safety Executive (HSE).

In this publication, each regulation is reproduced, followed by any associated ACOP which the Health and Safety Commission (HSC) has approved under section 16 of the Health and Safety at Work etc Act 1974, and other guidance on compliance.

For convenience, the text of the Regulations is given in *ITALIC* type, with the ACOP in **BOLD** type and accompanying guidance in NORMAL type.

Reference in this Code of Practice to another document does not imply approval by HSC of that document except to the extent necessary to give effect to this Code. A list of standards, ACOPs and guidance referred to in this publication is given in Appendix 4.

The ACOP/guidance is written in general terms; it should be used in conjunction with the more detailed advice in referenced publications. In this ACOP/guidance, cross-references to specific paragraphs are references to other parts of this publication, unless otherwise stated. Information on meanings of terms is given later in this Introduction, under the heading 'Terms used in Regulations and ACOP/guidance'.

Content and scope of Regulations

The Regulations deal with the safe installation, maintenance and use of gas systems, including gas fittings, appliances and flues, mainly in domestic and commercial premises, eg offices, shops, public buildings and similar places. They update, consolidate and replace the Gas Safety (Installation and Use) Regulations 1994 and subsequent amending Regulations. The Regulations generally apply to any 'gas' as defined in the Gas Act 1986 (amended by the Gas Act 1995), apart from any gas comprising wholly or mainly of hydrogen when used in non-domestic premises. The requirements therefore include both natural gas and liquefied petroleum gas (LPG), subject to certain exceptions, eg regulation 37 (escape of gas) generally excludes natural gas (which is covered by similar provisions under the Gas Safety (Management) Regulations 1996).

The Regulations place responsibilities on a wide range of people, including those installing, servicing, maintaining or repairing gas appliances and other gas fittings; as well as suppliers and users of gas, including certain landlords. They cover a wide variety of premises and gas systems/appliances, but certain exceptions are provided, for example see definitions and interpretation in regulation 2(1)–(7), and provisions concerning application/exceptions from requirements under specific regulations.

The enforcing authority for the Regulations is HSE or the relevant local authority, as determined in the particular circumstances by the Health and Safety (Enforcing Authority) Regulations 1998.

Summary of requirements

This summary is for background only and is intended to provide a general indication of some of the main requirements. It should not be taken as a statement of the legal position, for which reference needs to be made to the relevant statutory instrument (SI 1998 No 2451).

These Regulations, subject to certain exceptions/provisos:

- require work on a gas fitting to be carried out only by a competent person; and employers of gas fitting operatives, together with other specified persons (eg those in control of the work such as building contractors), to ensure that operatives have the required competence for the particular work being done. Employers of persons carrying out work on gas fittings/service pipework and self-employed persons doing this work are required to be a member of a class of persons approved by HSE; at the time of publication of this ACOP/guidance this means that they should be registered with the Gas Safe Register (regulation 3);
- require any employer or self-employed person requiring work to be done on a gas fitting, or in control to any extent of such work (eg a contractor), to take steps to ensure the person doing the work is, or is employed by a member of a class of persons approved by HSE (regulation 4);
- require an installer of a gas fitting to ensure that the fitting is suitable for the purpose for which it is to be used. Installation of lead pipe/fittings is prohibited and controls are placed on the use of non-metallic pipe/fittings. Any work on a gas fitting/storage vessel is required to comply with appropriate standards and to be done in a manner which avoids danger to any person (regulation 5);
- specify measures to be taken by any person working on a gas fitting against danger from gas release, and requirements for sealing gasways and testing gastightness after work is completed. Use of ignition sources is prohibited where there is a risk of fire/explosion, eg in searching for a gas leak. Requirements are specified for safe installation of gas (eg LPG) storage vessels, and the storage of natural gas at domestic premises is prohibited (regulation 6);
- require gas fittings to be protected from damage, including corrosion, and from blockage by a foreign body, eg dirt/dust (regulation 7);
- prohibit any alteration to premises in which a gas fitting or storage vessel is installed which causes the fitting or storage vessel no longer to comply with the Regulations, as well as work on a gas fitting or associated flue/ventilation system which results in danger to any person (regulation 8);
- require an emergency control to be provided when gas is first supplied to premises. Where this control is not adjacent to a meter, a notice is required to be posted adjacent to the control, describing the procedure in event of a gas escape (regulation 9);
- require electrical continuity to be maintained during work on a gas fitting, where necessary to avoid danger (regulation 10);
- require gas meters to be installed so as to avoid, as far as is reasonably practicable, adverse effect on means of escape from premises, and specify requirements concerning construction of certain meters. Other requirements are imposed for meter installation, eg to avoid electrical hazards and facilitate inspection/maintenance, and for pipe connections, gastightness tests and purging of meters (regulations 11–12);
- specify requirements for meter housings concerning safe dispersal of any gas escape, avoidance of combustible materials, and provision of keys to enable consumer access (regulation 13);
- stipulate protection arrangements to maintain gas pressure within safe limits, in the case of systems supplied from gas (eg LPG) storage tanks, or from certain cylinder configurations. Requirements are also included for sealing of regulators against unauthorised interference (regulation 14);

- require an emergency notice to be posted at a primary meter, giving the procedure to be adopted in event of a gas escape; a notice showing the position of the emergency control is also required in certain cases (regulation 15);
- prohibit installation of a prepayment meter as a primary meter in certain cases and specify requirements for notices at primary meters where gas is supplied to more than one secondary meter. Precautions, eg for isolation/sealing, are also specified for situations where a primary meter has been removed (regulation 16);
- require any person supplying or permitting the supply of gas through a primary meter to a secondary meter (eg a landlord), to display at specified positions, a notice showing the configuration of the gas system (regulation 17);
- require installation pipework to be installed in a safe position having regard to factors which might affect safety, eg location of other pipes, drains, cables and electrical apparatus. Any person connecting installation pipework to a meter is required to inform the person responsible for the premises (eg the occupier) of the need for equipotential bonding (regulation 18);
- specify restrictions and protective measures for pipes passing through solid walls and floors, cavity walls and building foundations; conditions are stipulated whereby pipework associated with 'living flame effect fires' may be run in a wall cavity. Ducts and voids accommodating installation pipework are required to be adequately ventilated (regulation 19);
- require installation pipework to be installed so as to avoid impairing the structure or fire resistance of a building (regulation 20);
- require a receptor to be fitted to installation pipework where liquid or solid deposits may occur, eg from 'wet gas' (regulation 21);
- specify requirements for gastightness testing after work has been done on installation pipework, and for purging/sealing of such pipework both in cases where gas is being supplied to the premises where it is installed, and where gas is not being so supplied (regulation 22);
- require installation pipework, other than in premises or part of premises used only as a dwelling or living accommodation, to be marked, eg colour coded, in any position accessible to inspection, to identify that it is carrying gas (regulation 23);
- require a valve to be fitted in certain installation pipework and a system diagram provided (eg for use by emergency services), where service pipe/pipework exceeding specified sizes feeds certain buildings or floor areas (regulation 24);
- require any person installing a gas appliance to ensure it is safe for use; is not left connected to the gas supply unless it can be used safely; it complies with other relevant safety requirements (eg gas appliances safety legislation), and that any second-hand appliance is in a safe condition for further use. Any work on an appliance is required to maintain safety standards and requirements are specified for the examination of any appliance after work has been done, and for notification of any defect to the owner/user (regulation 26);
- require any flue to be suitable and in a proper condition for safe operation of the appliance which it serves, and any power-operated flue system to prevent operation of the appliance if the draught fails. Requirements to enable inspection of, and to prevent spillage of combustion products from, certain flues are specified; and any flue is required to be installed in a safe position (regulation 27);
- require a gas appliance to be installed in a position readily accessible for operation, inspection and maintenance (regulation 28);
- require the installer of a gas appliance to leave the manufacturer's instructions for the appliance, for use by the owner or occupier of the premises where the appliance is installed (regulation 29);
- prohibit installation of certain gas appliances in specified rooms unless the appliance is room-sealed. In other specified locations, certain appliances are required to be room-sealed or fitted with a device to cause shutdown

before a dangerous quantity of combustion products can build up in the room concerned; a general prohibition is placed on the installation of any instantaneous water heater, unless it is room-sealed or fitted with such a device (regulation 30);
- prohibit installation of suspended appliances unless the installation pipework is capable of supporting the weight imposed and the appliance is designed to be so supported (regulation 31);
- specify requirements for interlocking of automatic flue dampers, and their inspection. Installation of a manual flue damper on a domestic appliance is prohibited, and where an appliance is installed to an existing flue incorporating a manual flue damper, the damper is required to be permanently fixed in the open position (regulation 32);
- specify requirements for testing gastightness and examining appliances, flues, ventilation etc, and action where adjustments are necessary; in cases where a gas appliance is installed at a time when gas is being supplied to the premises concerned. Requirements are also specified where installation takes place when gas is not being supplied to premises (regulation 33);
- require a responsible person for any premises (for instance, the occupier/ owner of the premises, eg landlord) not to use or permit the use of any unsafe appliance. Persons carrying out specified work, eg on service pipes or gas fittings, are required to report any appliance they suspect as being dangerous to the responsible person for the premises, or where this person is not available, to the gas supplier or transporter, as appropriate (regulation 34);
- require an employer or self-employed person to ensure that any gas appliance, flue or installation pipework installed at a place of work they control is maintained in a safe condition (regulation 35);
- require landlords, in specified circumstances, to ensure safe maintenance of gas appliances, flues and installation pipework installed in premises under their control, that annual safety checks are carried on such appliances/flues and that a record is kept and issued (or in certain cases, displayed) to tenants. Landlords are required to ensure that no gas fitting of a type that would contravene regulation 30 (eg certain instantaneous water heaters) is fitted in any room occupied or to be occupied as sleeping accommodation after the Regulations came into force. This includes any room converted into such accommodation after that time (regulation 36);
- specify action to be taken by gas suppliers and persons responsible for premises in event of an escape of gas other than natural gas (as covered by the Gas Safety (Management) Regulations 1996); this extends to the emission of, or suspected emission of, carbon monoxide from an appliance using gas, other than natural gas supplied from a network (regulation 37);
- require protective measures as stipulated by the gas transporter, to be taken by a consumer where gas is used with plant (such as a compressor or engine) liable to cause dangerous fluctuation of pressure in the gas supply, or where an extraneous gas (eg compressed air) is used in connection with the consumption of gas (regulation 38).

Interface with other safety legislation

The Regulations have an interface with requirements under other legislation, as referred to in this ACOP/guidance. This includes:

- Health and Safety at Work etc Act 1974 (HSW Act);
- Gas Acts 1986 and 1995 (GA);
- Pipelines Safety Regulations 1996 as amended (PSR);
- Pressure Equipment Regulations 1999 as amended;
- Gas Safety (Management) Regulations 1996 (GSMR);
- Workplace (Health, Safety and Welfare) Regulations 1992 (WHSR);

- Management of Health and Safety at Work Regulations 1999 (MHSWR);
- Provision and Use of Work Equipment Regulations 1998 (PUWER);
- Gas Appliances (Safety) Regulations 1995 (GASR);
- Construction (Design and Management) Regulations 2007 (CDM);
- Pressure Systems Safety Regulations 2000 (PSSR);
- Health and Safety (Safety Signs and Signals) Regulations 1996 (SSR);
- Building Regulations and Building Standards (Scotland) Regulations;
- Dangerous Substances and Explosive Atmospheres Regulations 2002.

Brief summaries of these provisions and details of ACOPs and guidance are given in Appendices 3 and 4, respectively. It is important to recognise that requirements under GSIUR operate within the overall framework of safety controls imposed by the HSW Act and MHSWR on employers and self-employed persons generally. Under those provisions, any gas engineering business needs to ensure that hazards associated with work on gas fittings are properly identified, risks assessed, and suitable control measures are put into place. MHSWR requires employers to make appropriate arrangements for effective planning, organisation, control, monitoring and review of the preventive and protective measures in place, eg to comply with GSIUR and the HSW Act obligations (see Appendix 3).

In the case of workplaces, certain requirements in GSIUR (eg concerning notices, marking of pipes, and precautions to avoid risk to persons during work on a gas system) may interface, directly or indirectly, with provisions in respect of safety signs under SSR – see Appendices 3 and 4.

Terms used in Regulations and ACOP/guidance

Words and expressions which are defined in the Health and Safety at Work etc Act 1974 and the Management of Health and Safety at Work Regulations 1999 have the same meaning in this Code of Practice and guidance unless the context otherwise requires.

Any reference to an 'appropriate standard' is a reference to any of the following which are current at the time of the work activity:

- a British Standard (see Appendix 4);
- a relevant standard or code of practice of a national standards body of any member state of the European Union (EU);
- a relevant technical specification acknowledged for use as a standard by a public authority of any member state of the EU;
- traditional procedures of manufacture of a member state of the EU where these are the subject of a written technical description sufficiently detailed to permit assessment of the goods or materials for the use specified;
- a specification sufficiently detailed to permit assessment for goods or materials of an innovative nature (or subject to innovative process of manufacture such that they cannot comply with a recognised standard or specification) and which will fill the purpose provided by the specified standard;

provided that the proposed standard, code of practice, technical specification or procedure of manufacture provides, in use, equivalent levels of safety, suitability and fitness for purpose to those achieved by the standard to which it is expressed to be equivalent.

The mutual recognition in the previous paragraph is also extended to products originating in European Economic Area member states who are contracting parties to the Agreement on the European Economic Area (EEA), which conform to the standards, regulations, specifications or traditional procedures of manufacture legally applied in those states and which offer an equivalent standard of safety to that required in GSIUR.

The definitions of some terms in GSIUR, eg 'distribution main', 'emergency control', 'gas fittings', 'installation pipework', 'service pipe' and 'service valve' are also used in the Pipelines Safety Regulations 1996 and the Gas Safety (Management) Regulations 1996. Certain terms, eg 'service pipe', 'gas consumer' etc, are also used in the Gas Act 1986 (as amended) where meanings may differ slightly from those in GSIUR. However, this has no effect on how the provisions of the respective legislation, such as those concerning maintenance of pipes/pipework, are applied.

The terms 'gas engineer' and 'engineer' are not defined in GSIUR but are used in the guidance and ACOP; in this context they mean any person who carries out work on a gas system or gas storage vessel. This includes (but is not restricted to) any person who installs, services, maintains, connects, reconnects, disconnects, removes or repairs gas appliances or other fittings whether they are an employer, employee, self-employed or working on their own behalf, ie in 'do-it-yourself' activity.

The ACOP and guidance refers in several places to the requirement (under regulation 3(3)) for any gas engineering business to be in membership of a class of persons approved by HSE, and in that context, registration with Gas Safe Register is specified, as an example. This approach reflects the situation at the time of publication of this ACOP/guidance, where the only class of persons approved by HSE is the Gas Safe Register. However, it also recognises that another registration body could be appointed at some time in the future (see paragraph 44). For ease of reference, the term Gas Safe-registered engineer, is used in the ACOP/guidance and this should be taken to include a registered gas installation business (whether an employer or self-employed) or an operative employed by a registered gas engineering business.

For the purposes of this publication, where appliance standards refer to domestic use, this should be taken as reference to the type of appliance rather than the location. A small cooker in an office canteen would therefore normally be regarded as a domestic-type appliance in this context.

The term 'gas system' as used in the ACOP/guidance means all gas installation pipework, fittings and appliances as well as the provision of ventilation and flueing. Any reference to a 'secondary meter' includes a 'sub-deduct meter' (see paragraph 131); and unless the context otherwise requires, reference to 'Building Regulations' means Regulations currently in force in England and Wales as well those applicable in Scotland (see Appendix 3).

Typical installations

Diagrams of typical installations are given in Appendix 5. However, it must be stressed that these are only general illustrations and variations may occur in specific circumstances.

Carbon monoxide (CO) alarms

CO alarms are a useful back-up precaution but must not be regarded as a substitute for proper installation and maintenance of gas equipment by a Gas Safe registered engineer. Such alarms should comply with BS EN 50291 and carry the appropriate conformity marking. CO alarms should be installed, checked and serviced in accordance with manufacturer's instructions.

Application of Regulations to the apparently self-employed

Although only the courts can give an authoritative interpretation of the law, in considering the application of these Regulations and ACOP/guidance to persons working under another's direction, the following should be considered:

If people working under the control and direction of others are treated as self-employed for tax and national insurance purposes, they are nevertheless treated as their employees for health and safety purposes. It may therefore be necessary to take appropriate action to protect them. If any doubt exists about who is responsible for the health and safety of a worker this could be clarified and included in the terms of the contract. However, remember, a legal duty under the HSW Act cannot be passed on by means of a contract and there will still be duties towards others under section 3 of the HSW Act. If such workers are employed on the basis that they are responsible for their own health and safety, legal advice should be sought before doing so.

PART A GENERAL

Regulation 1

Citation and commencement

(1) These Regulations may be cited as the Gas Safety (Installation and Use) Regulations 1998 and shall come into force on 31 October 1998.

Regulation 2

General interpretation and application

1   This regulation defines important terms used in GSIUR. These definitions, together with regulation 2(2)–(7) (application/interpretation), largely determine how requirements are applied in particular circumstances (see paragraphs 2–42).

(1) In these Regulations, unless the context otherwise requires -

"appropriate fitting" means a fitting which -

(a) has been designed for the purpose of effecting a gas tight seal in a pipe or other gasway,
(b) achieves that purpose when fitted, and
(c) is secure, so far as is reasonably practicable, against unauthorised opening or removal;

2   Use of an 'appropriate fitting' is required in several regulations (eg 6(2), 6(3), 16(3), 22(2), 22(3), 22(5), 33(2) and 33(3)) for sealing-off a gasway (ie a passage through which gas may pass) in order to prevent escape of gas, such as from open-ended pipework following disconnection of an appliance, or to seal-off the supply of gas to an appliance pending completion of work and safe commissioning. Any such fitting should be designed for the purpose (ie not improvised from whatever is at hand, such as a fitting intended to seal other pipework, eg water pipes), and should comply with appropriate standards (see Appendix 4). For instance, suitable screw-in or soldered fittings should be used which securely blank or cap-off open ends of pipes or incomplete gasways in appliances; conventional isolation valves or consumer emergency controls, which might readily be opened by an unauthorised person, must not be used for this purpose.

"distribution main" means any main through which a transporter is for the time being distributing gas and which is not being used only for the purpose of conveying gas in bulk;

"emergency control" means a valve for shutting off the supply of gas in an emergency; being a valve intended for use by a consumer of gas;

3   The emergency control is a valve intended, and readily accessible, for use by the consumer, ie end-user, of gas. For example, a valve located in a meter-room which is locked (for security), and accessible only to a landlord, gas supplier, gas transporter and/or emergency services, cannot be regarded as an 'emergency control'. Where a meter is fitted, the meter control valve may be used as the emergency control, subject to certain conditions – see regulation 9(1) and paragraph 92.

4   Although there may be more than one emergency control serving a particular premises, it is the outlet of the first emergency control downstream of the distribution main which marks the interface between a 'service pipe' and 'installation pipework' (see definition of 'service pipe' below). There is a similar

Guidance 2

interface in other related legislation, eg the Pipelines Safety Regulations 1996 (see the relevant paragraph under 'Terms used in Regulations and ACOP/guidance' in the Introduction).

Regulation 2

"flue" means a passage for conveying the products of combustion from a gas appliance to the external air and includes any part of the passage in a gas appliance duct which serves the purpose of a flue;

Guidance 2

5 Flues come in many forms; they can be natural draught or fan-assisted, open or room-sealed, single or shared, or various combinations of these. For example, they can range from a simple individual natural draught flue to the more complex shared room-sealed natural draught (eg U- or Se-duct). Further information on types of flue design is given in appropriate standards (see Appendix 4).

Regulation 2

"gas" means any substance which is or (if it were in a gaseous state) would be gas within the meaning of the Gas Act 1986$^{(a)}$ except that it does not include gas consisting wholly or mainly of hydrogen when used in non-domestic premises;

(a) 1986 c.44.

Guidance 2

6 The definition of 'gas' includes: (a) methane, ethane, propane, butane, hydrogen and carbon monoxide, (b) a mixture of two or more of these gases, and (c) a combustible mixture of one or more of these gases and air. A mixture mainly composed of (a), (b) or (c), and containing another gas (eg a flammable, non-flammable or inert gas not itself covered by the definition), is also included. However, any gas consisting wholly or mainly of hydrogen when used in non-domestic premises, eg a laboratory in the industrial or education sector, is excluded, as is any gas wholly comprised of a substance not listed in (a) above, such as acetylene, oxygen or nitrogen. The substances within the definition are covered irrespective of physical form, eg both liquid and gaseous phases are included (but see paragraph 8 below).

7 The Regulations therefore cover natural gas, LPG, methane from coal mines, landfill gas etc, when these products are stored, supplied or used in situations within the scope of GSIUR, eg see definition of 'gas fittings' and 'gas appliance', and regulation 2(4)–(7). Both situations where gas fittings are used in connection with gas (normally natural gas) conveyed to premises through a distribution main, and where they are used with gas (mainly LPG) supplied from a storage vessel are covered by the Regulations, see regulation 2(3).

8 Although the definition of gas includes certain liquefied gases, most situations where LPG is likely to be used in liquid form, eg for automotive use or for grain drying, are not covered by these Regulations – see regulation 2(4)–(6).

Regulation 2

"gas appliance" means an appliance designed for use by a consumer of gas for heating, lighting, cooking or other purposes for which gas can be used but it does not include a portable or mobile appliance supplied with gas from a cylinder, or the cylinder, pipes and other fittings used for supplying gas to that appliance, save that, for the purposes of regulations 3, 35 and 36 of these Regulations, it does include a portable or mobile space heater supplied with gas from a cylinder, and the cylinder, pipes and other fittings used for supplying gas to that heater;

Guidance 2

9 The definition includes a wide range of appliances fuelled by gas. It is implicit that gas has to be stored, supplied or used (basically as a fuel gas) to be covered by the Regulations. The venting to atmosphere of waste gas from coal mines, landfill sites etc is therefore not covered. However, where recovered vent gas from these places is used in appliances at premises subject to the Regulations, it is covered.

Guidance

10 The supply of gas to the propulsion system of any vehicle does not come within the scope of the Regulations (see exception in regulation 2(6)). Therefore, LPG or natural gas powered vehicles, including fork-lift trucks etc, do not need to conform to these Regulations.

11 Mobile/portable appliances, where gas is supplied from a cylinder, are not generally covered. However, a mobile or portable space heater, such as an air heater, gas fire or convector, which is supplied with gas from a cylinder is subject to regulations 3, 35 and 36 (provided it is in premises covered by the Regulations). For instance, this means that appliances such as LPG cabinet heaters provided by landlords are required to be properly maintained, and checked for safety at least once per year by a person who is, or is employed by, a member of a class of persons approved by HSE under regulation 3, eg a Gas Safe-registered gas engineer (see regulations 3, 35 and 36). Work (eg servicing or maintenance) of any gas appliance, including a mobile or portable space heater, where carried out at premises generally excluded from GSIUR, such as factories, is not covered, irrespective of whether the appliance is intended for use in situations within the scope of the Regulations; subject to the requirements in regulation 3(8) concerning work on gas fittings in certain vehicles, vessels or caravans, see also paragraph 49. However, similar safety controls under separate legislation may apply in circumstances not covered by GSIUR (see paragraph 42).

Regulation

"gas fittings" means gas pipework, valves (other than emergency controls), regulators and meters, and fittings, apparatus and appliances designed for use by consumers of gas for heating, lighting, cooking or other purposes for which gas can be used (other than the purpose of an industrial process carried out on industrial premises), but it does not mean -

(a) any part of a service pipe;
(b) any part of a distribution main or other pipe upstream of the service pipe;
(c) a gas storage vessel; or
(d) a gas cylinder or cartridge designed to be disposed of when empty;

Guidance

12 This definition effectively excludes from the Regulations any gas fitting which is part of an industrial process carried out on industrial premises, eg gas fired industrial process plant and furnaces. The exclusion extends to industrial premises not covered by the exceptions (eg concerning factories, mines and quarries) in regulation 2(4); this means, for instance, that bitumen boilers and welding torches are not covered by the Regulations even where they are used at construction sites and similar places which may otherwise fall within scope (see also paragraphs 29–30). Although control devices primarily intended for use by the consumer, eg knobs and switches for controlling the heat or temperature functions of the appliance, are covered by the definition, work on such devices is generally excluded from the Regulations (regulation 2(6)(c) refers). The definition of 'gas fittings' excludes any service pipe (eg as in a network supplying natural gas), but covers service pipework, such as used in the supply of gas from an LPG storage vessel.

Regulation

"gas storage vessel" means a storage container designed to be filled or re-filled with gas at the place where it is connected for use or a re-fillable cylinder designed to store gas, and includes the vapour valve; but it does not include a cylinder or cartridge designed to be disposed of when empty;

"gas water heater" includes a gas fired central heating boiler;

"installation pipework" means any pipework for conveying gas for a particular consumer and any associated valve or other gas fitting including any pipework

Regulation 2

used to connect a gas appliance to other installation pipework and any shut off device at the inlet to the appliance, but it does not mean -

(a) a service pipe;
(b) a pipe comprised in a gas appliance;
(c) any valve attached to a storage container or cylinder; or
(d) service pipework;

Guidance 2

13 Installation pipework generally connects a meter or emergency control valve to a gas appliance. It includes pipework used to connect an appliance to other installation pipework (ie an 'appliance connector') and any shut-off device, eg isolation valve, at the inlet to the appliance (regulation 26(6) refers). However, any pipe comprised in a gas appliance, ie forming an integral part of an appliance, is excluded. See diagrams of typical installations in Appendix 5.

Regulation 2

"meter by pass" means any pipe and other gas fittings used in connection with it through which gas can be conveyed from a service pipe or service pipework to installation pipework without passing through the meter;

"primary meter" means the meter nearest and downstream of a service pipe or service pipework for ascertaining the quantity of gas supplied through that pipe or pipework by a supplier;

"re-fillable cylinder" means a cylinder which is filled other than at the place where it is connected for use;

"the responsible person", in relation to any premises, means the occupier of the premises or, where there is no occupier or the occupier is away, the owner of the premises or any person with authority for the time being to take appropriate action in relation to any gas fitting therein;

"room-sealed appliance" means an appliance whose combustion system is sealed from the room in which the appliance is located and which obtains air for combustion from a ventilated uninhabited space within the premises or directly from the open air outside the premises and which vents the products of combustion directly to open air outside the premises;

Guidance 2

14 The definition of 'room-sealed appliance' is of key importance in the context of regulation 30 which imposes restrictions on types of appliances which may be installed in certain accommodation. In this definition, the term 'premises' refers to the building or structure in which the appliance is located. The definition includes appliances where combustion air is drawn from an uninhabited space, but this option would be precluded for separate safety reasons (and would contravene GSIUR) in certain situations, eg in boats where air may not be drawn from petrol engine spaces.

15 The term 'room-sealed appliance' covers a wide range of appliances, both natural and fanned draught, including those connected to shared flues, eg U- and Se-duct, and 'vertex' systems – see appropriate standards (Appendix 4). The definition requires combustion products to be vented directly to open air outside premises; openings should therefore be avoided in any flue serving such an appliance (ie throughout its length inside any building), apart from any opening which is integral and essential to the correct operation of the flue, purpose-designed and properly located for its application (eg a 'vertex' flue in a loft space). It may be necessary to fit a guard around any such flue opening to prevent possible ignition of nearby combustible materials (see also paragraph 5 and Appendix 1).

Regulation 2

"service pipe" means a pipe for distributing gas to premises from a distribution main, being any pipe between the distribution main and the outlet of the first emergency control downstream from the distribution main;

Guidance 2

16 Although some of the regulations apply to service pipes, detailed requirements for these pipes are covered by the Pipelines Safety Regulations 1996 (see Appendix 3). Certain duties, eg concerning maintenance of service pipes, are also imposed under the Gas Act 1986 (as amended by the Gas Act 1995), see the relevant paragraph under 'Terms used in Regulations and ACOP/guidance' in the Introduction to this publication.

17 Service pipes are normally the property of the gas transporter, who needs to be notified before any work is performed on such pipes, including connecting or disconnecting a meter to a service pipe. At least 48 hours notice needs to be given to the gas transporter and, in certain circumstances, the meter owner (if different) also needs to be notified, eg see Schedule 2B of the Gas Act 1986 (which was inserted by GA 1995).

Regulation 2

"service pipework" means a pipe for supplying gas to premises from a gas storage vessel, being any pipe between the gas storage vessel and the outlet of the emergency control;

"service valve" means a valve (other than an emergency control) for controlling a supply of gas, being a valve -

  (a) incorporated in a service pipe; and
  (b) intended for use by a transporter of gas; and
  (c) not situated inside a building;

"supplier" in relation to gas means -

  (a) a person who supplies gas to any premises through a primary meter; or
  (b) a person who provides a supply of gas to a consumer by means of the filling or re-filling of a storage container designed to be filled or re-filled with gas at the place where it is connected for use whether or not such container is or remains the property of the supplier; or
  (c) a person who provides gas in re-fillable cylinders for use by a consumer whether or not such cylinders are filled or re-filled directly by that person and whether or not such cylinders are or remain the property of that person, but a retailer shall not be deemed to be a supplier when he sells a brand of gas other than his own;

Guidance 2

18 Gas suppliers are subject to certain duties under the Regulations (eg to respond to a gas escape under regulation 37), and other regulations refer to the 'supplier of gas' in connection with duties placed on other persons (such as for notification of defective or dangerous appliances under regulations 26 and 34, respectively). The meaning of 'supplier' (and allocation of related responsibilities) depends on the specific circumstances, as determined by the definition in the Regulations; see paragraphs 19–21 below.

19 In the case of gas (primarily natural gas) supplied to premises through pipes, the 'supplier' is the person who supplies gas through the primary meter (who will also hold the licence required under section 7 of the Gas Act 1986 (as amended by GA1995)), and bills the consumer.

20 In the case of gas, eg LPG, supplied by filling a storage tank, or in cylinders, the meaning of 'supplier' depends on the circumstances:

Guidance

(a) Gas supplied direct to a consumer. Whether the supply is to a storage tank, or in cylinders, the 'supplier' is the 'gas company', whose gas is used to fill the tank or cylinders concerned – for the latter, this is normally the company specified on gas cylinders (see also paragraph (b)(ii) below).

(b) Gas supplied to an intermediate person, eg landlord, who provides a gas supply on to 'tenant' consumers. Allocation of 'supplier' duties is as follows:

(i) gas supplied by filling storage vessel. Where the gas is to be provided on by a landlord for the use of tenant(s) in a building or part of a building (eg flat), the LPG company is responsible (regulation 2(2)(b) provides an exception for the landlord in these circumstances). However, where the gas is provided for use by consumers in premises other than buildings, such as caravans, the landlord (eg caravan park operator) is the 'supplier';

(ii) gas supplied in cylinders. The gas company attracts supplier-related duties in all cases, but where the landlord provides the gas for use in premises other than buildings, eg caravans, mobile homes, residential park homes etc, duties are shared between the gas company and the landlord.

In all of the above situations, allocation of 'supplier' duties is not affected by who owns the storage tank or cylinders concerned. Furthermore, persons involved in intermediate activities only, eg road tanker operators, or retailers/contract fillers of LPG cylinders (who only handle gas of another company's brand), are not regarded as 'suppliers'.

21 Wherever duties are shared by different persons, close co-operation and clear definition of agreed responsibilities is essential, to ensure requirements are effectively met and there are no gaps in safety cover, eg concerning response to a gas escape. Although the meaning of 'supplier' provides the basis for allocating related duties under the Regulations, this does not prevent dutyholders making contractual arrangements, and regulation 37 specifically provides for a gas supplier to appoint another person/organisation to act as an 'emergency service provider' (see paragraph 240).

Regulation

"transporter" in relation to gas means a person who conveys gas through a distribution main;

"work" in relation to a gas fitting includes any of the following activities carried out by any person, whether an employee or not, that is to say -

(a) installing or re-connecting the fitting;
(b) maintaining, servicing, permanently adjusting, disconnecting, repairing, altering or renewing the fitting or purging it of air or gas;
(c) where the fitting is not readily movable, changing its position; and
(d) removing the fitting.

but the expression does not include the connection or disconnection of a bayonet fitting or other self-sealing connector.

Guidance

22 For the purposes of these Regulations, 'work' includes do-it-yourself activities, work undertaken as a favour for friends and relatives, and work for which there is no expectation of reward or gain, eg voluntary activity for charities. This means that anyone carrying out such work must have the necessary competence, as required by regulation 3(1). However, membership of an HSE approved class of persons (under regulation 3(3)) is required only by businesses carrying out gas fitting work (see paragraphs 43–45).

Guidance

23 The definition of 'work in relation to a gas fitting' lists specific activities covered by this term, but this list is not exclusive and other operations may also comprise 'work'. The definition is wide-ranging and includes activities that could affect in any way the level of gas safety of a gas fitting (whether new or existing, and whether or not it contains gas). The term is of basic importance in determining the application of 'work-related' requirements under the Regulations, some of which, eg competence requirements under regulation 3, also apply in respect of work on a gas storage vessel (see paragraphs 45 and 48). In the context of 'work', terms not otherwise defined in the Regulations bear their normal meaning. Installation may refer to either a new or used/second-hand appliance or fitting and is not limited to initial installation in particular premises, ie it includes reinstallation (eg following servicing/repair work which has involved removal of the appliance/fitting), see also regulation 26(3) and associated guidance. For the purpose of the definition of 'work', 'disconnecting' means physically detaching or uncoupling a fitting (ie which involves breaking into a gasway), rather than simply isolating it by means of a valve or similar device, and both 'connecting' and 'reconnecting' should be understood accordingly.

24 For the purpose of the definition of 'work', readily movable appliances include appliances such as laboratory Bunsen burners and mobile barbecues, which are readily portable. Other appliances, eg free-standing cookers connected by standard flexible hose, are not considered to be 'readily movable', but can be moved temporarily, eg to clean the space they normally occupy; this type of activity is not regarded as 'work' within the meaning of these Regulations. (Where an appliance is connected by means of a bayonet fitting, this will need to be disconnected before moving the appliance – such disconnection is also excluded from the definition of 'work', as is the connection or reconnection of this type of fitting. It may be necessary to detach a stability bracket; if so, this needs to be refitted when the appliance is returned to its original position.) Where an appliance which is not readily movable is repositioned permanently, this is regarded as 'work' for the purpose of the Regulations; see also guidance on meaning of 'install' in paragraph 23.

25 Lighting or relighting of an appliance burner/pilot light, eg after temporary disruption or isolation of the gas supply (such as when premises are vacated or gas cylinders are changed, or following operation of an over- or underpressure control device), does not itself comprise work. However, the resumption of a gas supply in these or other circumstances may involve 'work', eg where purging of any gas fitting or appliance of air or gas is carried out; but in certain cases the checks on appliances under regulation 26(9) are not required (see regulation 26(10) and paragraphs 172–174). Any interruption of the gas supply possibly caused by faulty or maladjusted equipment should be thoroughly investigated and remedial action taken, as necessary, in accordance with the requirements for 'work' under the Regulations.

26 Regulation 2(6)(c) provides an exception for certain work activities in relation to control devices primarily intended for use by the consumer, eg knobs and switches for controlling the heat or temperature functions of the appliance (see paragraph 38).

Regulation

(2) For the purposes of these Regulations -

(a) any reference to installing a gas fitting includes a reference to converting any pipe, fitting, meter, apparatus or appliance to gas use; and
(b) a person to whom gas is supplied and who provides that gas for use in a flat or part of premises let by him shall not in so doing be deemed to be supplying gas.

Guidance

27   Landlords providing gas for tenant's use in flats or parts of buildings are not 'gas suppliers' for the purpose of these Regulations and do not attract supplier-related responsibilities. However, the position may be different where the gas is for use in any premises which is not a building, eg a caravan (see also definition of 'supplier' in regulation 2(1) and associated guidance). Irrespective of who is the gas supplier, there are separate duties on landlords under regulation 36, eg requiring gas appliances, installation pipework and flues provided for tenants to be maintained in a safe condition and annual safety checks to be carried out on such appliances and flues (see paragraphs 208–227).

Regulation

(3)   Subject to paragraphs (4) and (5) below, these Regulations shall apply to or in relation to gas fittings used in connection with -

(a)   gas which has been conveyed to premises through a distribution main; or

(b)   gas conveyed from a gas storage vessel.

(4)   Save for regulations 37, 38 and 41 and subject to regulation 3(8), these Regulations shall not apply in relation to the supply of gas to, or anything done in respect of a gas fitting at, the following premises, that is to say -

(a)   a mine or quarry within the meaning of the Mines and Quarries Act 1954[a] or any place deemed to form part of a mine or quarry for the purposes of that Act;

(b)   a factory within the meaning of the Factories Act 1961[b]; or any place to which any provisions of the said Act apply by virtue of sections 123 to 126 of that Act;

(c)   agricultural premises, being agricultural land, including land being or forming part of a market garden, and any building thereon which is used in connection with agricultural operations;

(d)   temporary installations used in connection with any construction work within the meaning assigned to that phrase by regulation 2(1) of the Construction (Design and Management) Regulations 1994[c];

(e)   premises used for testing of gas fittings; or

(f)   premises used for the treatment of sewage,

but they shall apply in relation to such premises or part thereof used for domestic or residential purposes or as sleeping accommodation.

(5)   Nothing in these Regulations shall apply in relation to the supply of gas to, or anything done in respect of a gas fitting on -

(a)   a self-propelled vehicle except when such vehicle is -

(i)   hired out in the course of a business; or

(ii)   made available to members of the public in the course of a business carried on from that vehicle;

(b)   a sea-going ship;

(a)   1954 c.70.
(b)   1961 c.34.
(c)   S.I. 1994/3140; regulation 2(1) was amended by S.I. 1996/1513*

*   The Construction (Health, Safety and Welfare) Regulations 1996 were revoked by the Construction (Design and Management) Regulations 2007.

Regulation

(c) a vessel not requiring a national or international load line certificate except when such a vessel is -

(i) hired out in the course of a business;
(ii) made available to members of the public in the course of a business carried out from that vessel; or
(iii) used primarily for domestic or residential purposes;

(d) a hovercraft; or
(e) a caravan used for touring otherwise than when hired out in the course of a business.

(6) Nothing in these Regulations shall apply in relation to -

(a) the supply of gas to the propulsion system of any vehicle or to any gas fitting forming part of such propulsion system;
(b) the supply of gas to, or anything done in respect of a bunsen burner used in an educational establishment; or
(c) work in relation to a control device on a gas appliance if -

(i) the device is intended primarily for use by a consumer of gas; and
(ii) the work does not involve breaking into a gasway.

(7) These Regulations shall not apply in relation to a gas fitting used for the purpose of training gas fitting operatives in a college or other training establishment, except that paragraphs (1) to (5) and (7) of regulation 3 shall apply to work in relation to a gas fitting carried out by a person providing such training.

(8) These Regulations shall not apply in relation to a gas fitting used for the purpose of assessing the competence of a gas fitting operative at an assessment centre where such assessment is carried out for the purposes of a nationally accredited certification scheme, except that regulation 3(1) and (2) shall apply to work in relation to a gas fitting carried out by a person carrying out such assessment.

Guidance

Premises covered by Regulations

28 For the purpose of these Regulations (except where the context otherwise requires, eg see regulation 2(2)(b)), 'premises' has the meaning given in section 53 of the Health and Safety at Work etc Act 1974. It covers any place, including any installation on land, the foreshore, offshore installations (whether floating or otherwise – but only within Great Britain (GB)), and any marquees or other movable structures. The Regulations therefore cover everywhere in GB, subject to the exceptions for vehicles, ships/boats, factories, agricultural land, construction installations, quarries, mines and other premises/situations in regulation 2(4)–(8). In particular, the Regulations cover gas systems and appliances in houses, flats, shops, offices, other commercial premises, and holiday accommodation, eg chalets and certain caravans, mobile homes and boats on inland waterways (see paragraphs 29–35).

29 Exceptions are provided for certain premises under regulations 2(4)–(6) as follows:

(a) regulation 2(4). The places mentioned, eg factories, mines and agricultural premises, are generally excluded, but regulations 37 (gas escapes) and 38 (antifluctuators and valves) do apply and regulation 3(8) specifically covers places where certain caravans and inland waterway boats are manufactured (see paragraph 49). Regulation 2(4)(b) excludes certain places, eg docks and

Guidance

electrical power stations, regarded as 'factories' under sections 123–126 of the Factories Act 1961. However, gas installation work that forms part of a construction activity (also treated as a 'notional' factory under the 1961 Act), eg installation of gas fittings/appliances in buildings being constructed for residential, industrial or commercial use, is covered with the exception of that in relation to fittings/appliances used in temporary installations such as site huts.

(b) regulation 2(5)–(6). The vehicles, ships, boats and other situations/activities mentioned are fully excluded from the Regulations.

30   The exceptions in regulations 2(4)–(6) cover any gas appliance or fitting (whether fixed or portable) in the premises concerned, irrespective of whether the fitting/appliance is intended for use in a place covered by the Regulations. The range of situations where industrial gas fittings are excluded is further extended (eg to certain other construction situations) by the exclusion for these fittings in the definition of 'gas fittings' (see paragraph 12). However, it must be stressed that where there are exclusions from these Regulations, similar requirements for gas safety may be applied under separate legislation, eg the Health and Safety at Work etc Act 1974 (see paragraph 42).

31   The exceptions in regulation 2(4) do not extend to domestic, residential or sleeping accommodation at the places specified. Therefore, the Regulations cover all such accommodation wherever it is found, apart from ships, boats, vehicles etc excluded under regulation 2(5). For example, caretakers' flats at factories or mines are covered.

32   Caravans used for touring which are hired out in the course of a business, and permanently sited caravans and mobile homes (hired out or otherwise) on holiday-home parks or similar sites, including farms, are covered. Similarly, any caravan used as an annexe to permanent accommodation, eg as a 'granny flat', or as temporary residential accommodation for employees (for instance on a construction site or farm), is covered by the Regulations.

33   The Regulations apply to certain boats not requiring a load line certificate, as specified in regulation 2(5)(c). These include boats (both permanently moored and those capable of navigation) which are hired out in the course of a business, eg boats used for holiday accommodation; any boat (including those privately-owned/occupied) used solely or primarily for domestic or residential purposes, such as houseboats and those used for cruising but in which the owner/user lives for most of the time; and boats made available to the public in the course of a business carried out from the vessel, eg floating restaurants and public houses. Privately owned boats used only for leisure or sporting purposes and not hired out in the course of a business are excluded, as are other 'inland waterway boats' not specified in regulation 2(5)(c), eg such boats used as a workplace by an employee of an inland waterway authority for canal repair/clearance purposes etc. Boats requiring a national or international load line certificate (ie broadly, seagoing cargo carrying ships) are also excluded from the Regulations, even where used on inland waterways.

34   Vessels subject to these Regulations will often fall outside the scope of merchant shipping legislation (MSL), ie because they are permanently-moored and/or not used for commercial purposes, but in some cases, such as commercially-operated pleasure boats (eg hire boats) and certain passenger vessels, these Regulations and MSL apply together; similarly additional requirements (including gas safety) may be applied by the navigation authority for the waters on which the vessel operates, for example the Boat Safety Scheme administered by the Environment Agency and British Waterways, as a condition of issuing licences for use of their waterways. In such situations, however, compliance with these

Guidance

Regulations will generally satisfy parallel requirements for gas safety under MSL or the relevant navigation authority scheme (see Appendix 4 for information on relevant Codes of Practice under MSL and 'boat safety' schemes in force when this ACOP was published).

35   Self-propelled vehicles hired out to, or frequented by the public, in the course of a business, eg motor caravans, are also covered. Mobile food 'stalls' (whether towed as 'caravans' or self-propelled) are covered; this includes such facilities where the public have access inside the vehicle or caravan concerned as well as 'serve through the hole' vendors. However, the tanks and associated fittings of any natural gas or LPG powered vehicles are excluded under regulation 2(6)(a), eg 'work' on such fittings is not covered (but other safety controls may apply in these circumstances – see paragraph 42).

Application in particular circumstances

36   Although the Regulations extend to a wide range of premises, not all uses of gas, or activities in relation to gas fittings/storage vessels are covered – see, for example, definitions of 'gas appliance', 'gas fittings, and 'work' under regulation 2(1). Furthermore, there are specific exceptions from requirements in particular regulations. These factors all need to be considered together in order to determine application of requirements in particular circumstances.

37   Appliances using non-refillable gas containers (eg some camping stoves, cigarette lighters, hairdressing curling tongs etc) are, for instance, not covered and other portable/mobile appliances are generally excluded, apart from space heaters and associated cylinders, pipes and fittings (which are subject to regulations 3, 35 and 36) – see definitions of 'gas storage vessel' and 'gas appliance', and paragraph 11.

38   Under regulation 2(6)(c), work on any control device associated with an appliance, which is primarily intended for use by the consumer (eg removal/replacement of electric thermostats and on/off timer switches) is excluded from the Regulations if this does not involve breaking into a gasway, ie where there is no risk of a gas escape. Persons carrying out such work are not, therefore, required to be in membership of an HSE approved class of persons, eg Gas Safe registered (see regulation 3), nevertheless competence to ensure any such work is done safely is required under the Health and Safety at Work etc Act 1974.

39   The exceptions in regulation 2(7)–(8) concerning gas fittings used in the training/assessment of gas fitting operatives recognise that these fittings may have deliberate faults introduced, eg to demonstrate specific problems or test fault-detection techniques. Most of the regulations, eg concerning appliance safety, do not apply in these circumstances but assessors/trainers are still required to possess the necessary competence to ensure safe conduct of such activities (this needs to take into account the level of trainee knowledge and experience, which might be limited) and training organisations also need to be in membership of an HSE approved class of persons, eg Gas Safe registered, under regulation 3(3)); the exception in regulation 2(7) is restricted to assessment for the purpose of a nationally accredited certification scheme (see paragraph 47) and therefore excludes other 'assessment' activities, eg checks and tests as part of the training of gas operatives.

40   Under regulation 2(7)–(8), both assessment and training organisations are required to ensure that their staff have the necessary competence (see regulation 3(2)), and in addition they need to meet obligations (eg under the Health and Safety at Work etc Act, Management of Health and Safety at Work Regulations, and Workplace (Health, Safety and Welfare) Regulations), for securing safety of

Guidance

both staff and trainees in these circumstances. For instance, this would include addressing activities involving 'faulty' appliances in the 'risk assessment' under MHSWR, and implementing the necessary control measures (eg by 'grading' work according to trainee experience, providing appropriate instructions and supervision and implementing formal procedures/checks to ensure gas fittings are left in a 'safe condition', after exercises have been completed).

41   The exceptions in regulation 2(7)–(8) do not cover gas fittings used for purposes other than training/assessment or those used in training or assessment of operatives at places other than training colleges or assessment centres, eg 'on the job' training/assessment carried out at different locations is subject to the Regulations in full.

Requirements at premises outside the Scope of the Regulations

42   Where there are exclusions under these Regulations, eg at factories, similar gas safety requirements may be applicable under the Health and Safety at Work etc Act 1974 and related legislation, eg the Workplace (Health, Safety and Welfare) Regulations 1992 and the Provision and Use of Work Equipment Regulations 1998 (see Appendix 3). In deciding whether these other, more general duties have been met in relation to installation and use of gas systems/appliances, the relevance of the more specific requirements of these Regulations will need to be considered.

PART B GAS FITTINGS – GENERAL PROVISIONS

Regulation 3

Qualification and supervision

(1) *No person shall carry out any work in relation to a gas fitting or gas storage vessel unless he is competent to do so.*

(2) *The employer of any person carrying out such work for that employer, every other employer and self-employed person who has control to any extent of such work and every employer and self-employed person who has required such work to be carried out at any place of work under his control shall ensure that paragraph (1) above is complied with in relation to such work.*

(3) *Without prejudice to the generality of paragraphs (1) and (2) above and subject to paragraph (4) below, no employer shall allow any of his employees to carry out any work in relation to a gas fitting or service pipework and no self-employed person shall carry out any such work, unless the employer or self-employed person, as the case may be, is a member of a class of persons approved for the time being by the Health and Safety Executive for the purposes of this paragraph.*

(4) *The requirements of paragraph (3) above shall not apply in respect of -*

(a) *the replacement of a hose or regulator on a portable or mobile space heater; or*
(b) *the replacement of a hose connecting a re-fillable cylinder to installation pipework.*

(5) *An approval given pursuant to paragraph (3) above (and any withdrawal of such approval) shall be in writing and notice of it shall be given to such persons and in such manner as the Health and Safety Executive considers appropriate.*

(6) *The employer of any person carrying out any work in relation to a gas fitting or gas storage vessel in the course of his employment shall ensure that such of the following provisions of these Regulations as impose duties upon that person and are for the time being in force are complied with by that person.*

(7) *No person shall falsely pretend to be a member of a class of persons required to be approved under paragraph (3) above.*

(8) *Notwithstanding sub-paragraph (b) of regulation 2(4), when a person is carrying out work in premises referred to in that sub-paragraph in relation to a gas fitting in a vehicle, vessel or caravan -*

(a) *paragraphs (1), (2) and (6) of this regulation shall be complied with as respects thereto; and*
(b) *he shall ensure, so far as is reasonably practicable, that the installation of the gas fittings and flues will not contravene the provisions of these Regulations when the gas fittings are connected to the gas supply,*

except that this paragraph shall not apply where the person has reasonable grounds for believing that the vehicle, vessel or caravan will be first used for a purpose which when so used will exclude it from the application of these Regulations by virtue of sub-paragraphs (a), (c) or (e) of regulation 2(5).

Guidance

43 All gas engineering businesses, including self-employed gas engineers, are (subject to the limited exceptions in regulation 3(4)) required to be in membership of a 'class of persons' approved by HSE, whether they carry out such work as their main or part activity. Gas engineers who are employed by a member of an approved 'class of persons', but who do separate work on their own behalf, need to be in membership of such class of persons, eg Gas Safe-registered, in their own right.

44 At the time of publication of this edition of this ACOP/guidance, the only body with such approval is the Gas Safe Register (www.gassaferegister.co.uk) (although other organisations may apply to HSE for consideration to act as a registration body if they so wish).

45 Anyone who does work on a gas fitting or gas storage vessel must be competent to do so, whether or not they are required to be a member of an approved class of persons. Therefore, do-it-yourself gas engineers and those performing favours for friends and relatives all need to have the required competence. The level and range of competence should match the full extent of work done, but needs only to be sufficient for and relevant to that work. Employers of gas fitting operatives are also required under regulation 3(2) to ensure that their employees have the required competence for the work undertaken; in addition to ensuring they are properly experienced and trained (see paragraph 47), this involves ongoing monitoring of performance standards, as necessary.

46 The duty to ensure gas engineers are competent extends to other employers and self-employed persons with control over the work concerned, eg certain contractors, and those requiring work to be done in a workplace under their control. Where there is more than one dutyholder in a particular situation, close liaison is essential to ensure requirements are met, eg through proper check procedures. Information on the scope of work a Gas Safe registered engineer is competent to perform may be obtained from the engineer certificate of competence (issued under the certification scheme referred to in paragraph 47) or where, under transitional registration arrangements, no certificate has yet been issued, from the Gas Safe Register – see also regulation 4 concerning duty to check for membership of an HSE approved class of persons.

47 Competence depends on a combination of training and experience. The ACOP *Standards of training in safe gas installation* provides guidance both on the scope of training and the need for proper assessment/reassessment of gas fitting operatives (see Appendix 4). Although failure to observe any provision of the Code is not in itself an offence, that failure may be taken by a Court in criminal proceedings as proof that a person has contravened a particular regulation. The ACOP extends to gas installation work at premises excluded from these Regulations but subject to the HSW Act sections 2 and 3 – see paragraph 42 and Appendix 3. The nationally accredited certification scheme introduced in January 1998 requires individual gas fitting operatives to have their competence assessed at five-yearly intervals by a certification body accredited by the United Kingdom Accreditation Service (UKAS).

48 Regulation 3 extends to work on portable or mobile space heaters, eg LPG cabinet heaters (where done at premises subject to the Regulations), see paragraph 11. As gas storage vessels are not 'gas fittings' within the meaning of these Regulations, the changing of cylinders, filling of storage tanks or fixing in position of such tanks does not require membership of an HSE approved class of persons, eg Gas Safe registration. However, people involved in these activities, or any of those covered by the exceptions in regulation 3(4)(a)–(b) (concerning certain 'like for like' hose/regulator replacement activities, such as where used/worn items

Guidance

are replaced) need to have the required competence and ensure that they follow instructions, eg given by the gas supplier/appliance manufacturer, as appropriate. Where other work is involved, eg installing or replacing an LPG tank requiring work on service pipework or other gas fitting(s), it should be carried out only by someone who is in membership of an HSE approved class of persons, eg a Gas Safe-registered engineer, with the required competence (see also regulation 2(6)(c) regarding exceptions for certain work on gas appliance control devices primarily intended for use by the consumer).

49   Regulation 3(8) requires manufacturers of caravans, holiday homes or inland waterway boats to be used in situations in which the Regulations will apply to ensure employees who install gas fittings (or who do subsequent maintenance or repair work) are competent, and to take reasonable steps to secure safety once their products are taken/retaken into use. Manufacturers should take reasonable steps, eg by arrangements with their supply outlets and dealers, to establish, as best they can, the intended use of their products and whether the requirements in regulation 3(8) will therefore apply. Whatever is the case, manufacturers also need to bear in mind other, more general, duties under health and safety and consumer protection legislation, and, in their own interests, it is recommended that they use the same standards of gas installation in all their products, and have quality control procedures to ensure that this is the case. In addition to the installation of gas fittings themselves, other relevant factors, eg location and size of flue and ventilation openings, need to be taken into account.

Regulation 4

Duty on employer

Regulation 4

Where an employer or self-employed person requires any work in relation to a gas fitting to be carried out at any place of work under his control or where an employer or self-employed person has control to any extent of work in relation to a gas fitting, he shall take reasonable steps to ensure that the person undertaking that work is, or is employed by, a member of a class of persons approved by the Health and Safety Executive under regulation 3(3) above.

ACOP 4

50   **Businesses should make reasonable efforts to obtain evidence that any person they intend to perform gas installation work (subject to regulation 3(3)), either under contract or on their own behalf, is a member, or employed by a member of a class of persons approved by HSE.**

Guidance

51   Regulation 4 applies to an employer/self-employed person requiring work to be done on an gas appliance/fitting installed at their workplace as well as to an employer or self-employed person having control over work done on a gas fitting, eg a contractor. The duty supplements that for checking competence under regulation 3(2) – see paragraphs 45-46.

52   At the time of publication of this ACOP/guidance, the 'class of persons' approved by HSE are those who are registered with the Gas Safe Register (see paragraph 44). The Gas Safe Register will provide evidence of registration and confirmation that any certificate of registration is still valid.

Regulation 5

Materials and workmanship

Regulation 5

(1)   No person shall install a gas fitting unless every part of it is of good construction and sound material, of adequate strength and size to secure safety and of a type appropriate for the gas with which it is to be used.

ACOP
5(1)

53 Gas engineers should acquaint themselves with the appropriate standards for gas fittings and ensure that the fittings they use are to those standards.

Guidance

54 Most new gas appliances used for domestic (eg cooking, heating and hot water production) purposes are subject to the Gas Appliances (Safety) Regulations 1995 and will carry the CE marking in addition to any recognised European standard mark and/or BSI kitemark. Some larger plant, eg for commercial use, will also bear the CE marking in conformity with other Regulations which implement EC directives, eg on machinery and pressure vessels.

55 Pipes should be of a suitable construction, material, strength and size to convey gas to the appliance and to ensure its safe operation; account needs to be taken of any special factors in particular circumstances, eg risk of physical damage to non-metallic pipework, for instance, from rodent attack (see also regulations 5(2) and 7)). Where the appropriate standard or manufacturer recommends a limited lifetime for a gas fitting (including plastic pipework), it should be replaced before the end of its limited life, unless it can be shown that continued use will not constitute a hazard. The manufacturer should be consulted, to establish whether the lifetime of the gas fitting can be extended, what tests need to be carried out, and the extended lifetime allowed. See also regulations 35–36 and associated guidance, concerning maintenance/safety check duties.

5(1)

Regulation

(2) Without prejudice to the generality of paragraph (1) above, no person shall install in a building any pipe or pipe fitting for use in the supply of gas which is -

(a) made of lead or lead alloy; or
(b) made of a non-metallic substance unless it is -

(i) a pipe connected to a readily movable gas appliance designed for use without a flue; or
(ii) a pipe entering the building and that part of it within the building is placed inside a metallic sheath which is so constructed and installed as to prevent, as far as is reasonably practicable, the escape of gas into the building if the pipe should fail.

5(2)

ACOP
5(2)

56 Non-metallic connectors for use with readily movable gas appliances should conform to the appropriate standard (see Appendix 4). Such hoses, pipes and pipe fittings need to be used only for the purpose for which they are designed.

Guidance

57 Appliances or meters may be connected to existing lead piping using suitable fittings, provided that the piping is in a safe condition, eg there is no sign of damage.

58 Apart from connectors to readily movable appliances such as Bunsen burners, non-metallic (eg plastic) pipes should only be used within buildings if sheathed in metal to minimise the risk of gas escaping if the pipe should fail. This requirement does not extend to polyethylene (PE) piping buried in ground beneath a building provided that the piping does not enter the building (but see regulation 19(5)). However, it does apply to that routed in spaces under floors. Plastic pipe fittings should not be used to seal pipes within buildings (see also definition of 'appropriate fitting' in regulation 2(1)). Although regulation 5(2) applies only to pipes and pipe fittings in buildings, it is recommended that a similar approach be adopted for other premises, eg caravans and inland waterway boats. See also regulation 26(2) concerning pipes for flued domestic appliances.

59 Free-standing gas cookers are generally movable, but are not regarded as 'readily movable' for the purpose of this regulation (see also paragraph 24).

5(2)

Guidance 5(2)

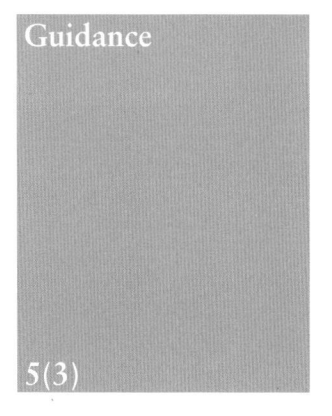

Flexible cooker hoses should therefore be of metallic construction; they should conform with appropriate standards and be used only for their intended purpose.

Regulation 5(3)

(3) No person shall carry out any work in relation to a gas fitting or gas storage vessel otherwise than in accordance with appropriate standards and in such a way as to prevent danger to any person.

Guidance 5(3)

60   This regulation covers two separate but related requirements. Work in relation to any gas fitting or gas storage vessel needs both to be in accordance with appropriate standards, and to be carried out in a manner which does not expose the gas engineer, or any other person, to danger, eg from a gas escape. It is the particular work being carried out which needs to comply with the appropriate standards; modifications completely unrelated to that work, eg upgrading to revised specifications, are not required (unless necessary to meet other provisions of the Regulations). The term 'appropriate standards' is not defined in the Regulations themselves, but a list of standards regarded as appropriate standards for the purpose of this ACOP and guidance is given in Appendix 4 (see also relevant paragraphs under 'Terms used in Regulations and ACOP/guidance' in the Introduction).

Regulation 6

General safety precautions

Regulation 6(1)–(2)

(1) No person shall carry out any work in relation to a gas fitting in such a manner that gas could be released unless steps are taken to prevent the gas so released constituting a danger to any person.

(2) No person carrying out work in relation to a gas fitting shall leave the fitting unattended unless every incomplete gasway has been sealed with the appropriate fitting or the gas fitting is otherwise safe.

ACOP 6(1)–(2)

61   Where work is carried out on a gas fitting that involves breaking into a gasway, it should be done in such a way that any resulting release of gas does not lead to danger. Where any gasway has been broken into, and the gas fitting concerned is to be left unattended before work is completed, the gasway should be sealed with an appropriate fitting so as to be gastight. Appropriate fitting(s) used to seal gasway(s) of an appliance should ensure that the gas supply to the appliance cannot be readily restored until safe to do so. Closure of an emergency control does not fulfil this requirement (see definition of 'appropriate fitting' in regulation 2(2)).

Guidance 6(1)–(2)

62   This regulation generally covers work done on existing gas fittings, including extension or modification of existing gas installations, that involves breaking into a live gasway. If the work has to be left unfinished for any significant period, during which appliances might be deliberately or inadvertently used, the gas supply to the (disconnected) appliance should be sealed, as specified in paragraph 61. Reference should be made to the requirements for an 'appropriate fitting' under the definition in regulation 2(1).

63   'Unattended' has differing meanings depending on the size of premises. For domestic premises it normally means that the person working on the gas system is absent from the premises for a significant time during which someone else (eg the appliance owner) could turn gas supply back on in order to use the appliance. For most larger commercial locations 'unattended' could mean being on another part of the site.

Regulation 6(3)

(3) Any person who disconnects a gas fitting shall, with the appropriate fitting, seal off every outlet of every pipe to which it was connected.

ACOP 6(3)

64 **The open-end(s) of any metal pipe(s) from which a gas fitting has been disconnected should be sealed with an appropriate metal fitting, see definition of 'appropriate fitting' in regulation 2(1).**

Guidance 6(3)

65 This regulation is largely intended to deal with situations in which gas appliances are removed, for instance because they are no longer needed or are being taken away when owners move home. When an appliance is disconnected and open-ended pipework is left, the pipework should always be left sealed with an appropriate fitting. A self-sealing coupling, eg on a cooker connection, does not need to be capped-off, except where there is a significant risk of interference (such as by a child). However, it should be checked that any disconnected coupling is not leaking gas (see paragraph 68), and any wall-mounted connector has been installed in the downward mounted position to prevent dirt or grit getting into the self-closing seal.

Regulation 6(4)

(4) No person carrying out work in relation to a gas fitting which involves exposing gasways which contain or have contained flammable gas shall smoke or use any source of ignition in such a manner as may lead to the risk of fire or explosion.

Guidance 6(4)

66 'Sources of ignition' include such tools as blow-lamps and hot-air guns. A safe system of work (including effective isolation of the gas supply etc) should be used to avoid any risk of fire or explosion; gasways should generally be purged of gas prior to the use of tools such as a blow torch.

Regulation 6(5)

(5) No person searching for an escape of gas shall use any source of ignition.

Guidance 6(5)

67 This prohibition extends to householders and other members of the general public.

68 The source of leaks should be located by sense of smell, gas detection instruments approved for use in flammable atmospheres, leak detection fluids, pressure test equipment or a combination of these methods.

Regulation 6(6)

(6) Where a person carries out any work in relation to a gas fitting which might affect the gas tightness of the gas installation he shall immediately thereafter test the installation for gas tightness at least as far as the nearest valves upstream and downstream in the installation.

ACOP 6(6)

69 **The gastightness of the installation should be tested in accordance with the appropriate standard.**

Guidance 6(6)

70 The pressure decay test, sometimes referred to as the gas soundness test or the pressure drop test for soundness, is often used for gastightness. In domestic situations the test normally needs to cover the installation pipework between the meter control valve or emergency control valve as appropriate, and the appliance shut-off device.

Regulation 6(7)

(7) No person shall install a gas storage vessel unless the site where it is to be installed is such as to ensure that the gas storage vessel can be used, filled or refilled without causing a danger to any person.

Guidance 6(7)

71 Guidance on installation of LPG vessels is given in UKLPG Codes of Practice (see Appendix 4).

Guidance 6(7)

72 LPG tanks should not be located indoors, within a bunded area or on a roof of a building. Location of LPG storage tanks should take into account the need for safe access for road tankers, where reasonable practicable with provision of off-road parking, and for safe delivery of LPG. Any LPG storage tank used to supply gas to multiple consumers should be located only at a site where the person providing the gas supply to consumers has full control over the access to the tank and associated equipment.

73 In Scotland, account should be taken of the restrictions imposed by the Building Regulations on the siting of LPG vessels (see Appendix 3).

Regulation 6(8)–(9)

(8) No person shall install in a cellar or basement:

(a) a gas storage vessel; or
(b) an appliance fuelled by liquefied petroleum gas which has an automatic ignition device or a pilot light.

(9) No person shall intentionally or recklessly interfere with a gas storage vessel or otherwise do anything which might affect a gas storage vessel so that the subsequent use of that vessel might cause a danger to any person.

Guidance 6(8)–(9)

74 The prohibitions extend to everyone, including householders and other members of the public.

75 The prohibitions in regulation 6(8) address the fire/explosion hazard, eg from possible leakage and accumulation of heavy LPG vapour in any cellar or basement or from involvement of a gas storage vessel in a building fire. Further guidance on the installation and maintenance of LPG installations is given in UKLPG Codes of Practice (see Appendix 4).

Regulation 6(10)

(10) No person shall store or keep gas consisting wholly or mainly of methane on domestic premises, and, for the purpose of this paragraph, such gas from time to time present in pipes or in the fuel tank of any vehicle propelled by gas shall be deemed not to be so stored or kept.

Guidance 6(10)

76 This regulation prohibits storage and keeping of natural gas at domestic premises, including for the purpose of home filling of gas-fuelled vehicles. However, this prohibition does not extend to natural gas in pipes, or in fuel tanks of parked or garaged vehicles. Similarly, equipment used for filling vehicle tanks is not prohibited where this does not involve storage, but any requirements stipulated by the gas transporter in relation to antifluctuators/valves need to be met in these circumstances, see regulation 38. The meaning of 'domestic premises' in regulation 6(10) is that given in section 53 of the Health and Safety at Work etc Act 1974 and includes any garden, yard or garage of such premises not used in common by the occupants of more than one such dwelling.

Regulation 7   Protection against damage

Regulation 7(1)

(1) Any person installing a gas fitting shall ensure that it is properly supported and so placed or protected as to avoid any undue risk of damage to the fitting.

ACOP 7(1)

77 **Gas fittings should be installed in accordance with appropriate standards.**

Guidance 7(1)

78 Gas fittings should be properly supported to ensure that no undue strain is placed upon them, eg by virtue of the weight or action of the gas fitting itself,

Guidance 7(1)

which could lead to failure or damage of the fitting (see also paragraph 188). Gas fittings should, as far as possible, be installed in a position which avoids any risk of damage from foreseeable activities in the vicinity, eg vehicular traffic. Where such risk cannot be avoided, fittings should be suitably protected against possible damage. This would need to be addressed, for instance, in the case of service pipework, meter installations and installation pipework, where location near to vehicular access routes cannot be avoided.

79 Details of suitable arrangements for support and protection of gas fittings are given in appropriate standards. Appliances need to be installed in accordance with manufacturer instructions; the Gas Appliances (Safety) Regulations 1995 require such instructions to accompany appliances supplied or placed on the market – see Appendix 3. Special care needs to be taken where a gas fitting is located in a movable structure such as a caravan or boat, to take account of wind, tides etc.

Regulation 7(2)

(2) No person shall install a gas fitting if he has reason to suspect that foreign matter may block or otherwise interfere with the safe operation of the fitting unless he has fitted to the gas inlet of, and any airway in, the fitting a suitable filter or other suitable protection.

Guidance 7(2)

80 Filters or other suitable protection may be necessary to protect against any adverse effect of dirt or dust. Such devices should be compatible with any connected appliance. If there is any doubt, the advice of the gas supplier/transporter and/or fitting manufacturer, as appropriate, needs to be sought.

Regulation 7(3)

(3) No person shall install a gas fitting in a position where it is likely to be exposed to any substance which may corrode gas fittings unless the fitting is constructed of materials which are inherently resistant to being so corroded or it is suitably protected against being so corroded.

Guidance 7(3)

81 Environments of particular concern are those where water, salt-spray, damp, corrosive chemicals or soot are present, or likely to be present. Special care needs to be taken where a gas fitting is located in a movable structure such as a boat, or a caravan on coastal sites. In some circumstances, it may be necessary to apply a protective coating but that coating should not affect safe operation of the fitting.

Regulation 8

Existing gas fittings

Regulation 8(1)

(1) No person shall make any alteration to any premises in which a gas fitting or gas storage vessel is fitted if that alteration would adversely affect the safety of the fitting or vessel in such a manner that, if the fitting or the vessel had been installed after the alteration, there would have been a contravention of, or failure to comply with, these Regulations.

Guidance 8(1)

82 This regulation embraces a wide range of physical alterations to premises that might affect the safety of an existing gas fitting or gas storage vessel installed in the premises where the alteration is to be made (see paragraph 87). Before a significant alteration is made to premises where a gas appliance is installed, eg installation or removal of windows, air bricks, extractor fan units etc, any implications for gas appliance/fitting safety need to be properly addressed (see paragraphs 83–87). Similarly, prior consideration needs to be given to the possible effect of any modification, such as a building extension, on the safety of a gas storage vessel (eg from any reduction in separation distances and standards of ventilation), or on service pipework (for example, the risk of damage to buried pipework from strain/weight imposed upon it) – see also regulations 6(7)–(8), 7(1) and 19(5). Requirements of Building Regulations, eg concerning ventilation and flues, should

Guidance

also be taken into account, as appropriate. Reference should also be made to regulation 36(11)–(12) concerning duties on landlords in respect of any room to be converted into sleeping accommodation.

83 Regulation 8(1) applies to householders, builders, gas engineers etc, and is supplementary to any requirements under the Construction (Design and Management) Regulations 2007. The implications of any change to premises for safety of a gas fitting or gas storage vessel need to be considered systematically as part of the overall work planning process.

84 In some cases, the effects of particular work for gas safety may be obvious. For example, where a chimney is being reduced in height or capped, its effectiveness in removing flue gases may be drastically affected. Before such work is started, it needs to be established whether, or not, the chimney is active and, if so, allowance made for this in the way the work is carried out. This may include planning for appliances to be disconnected before work commences, preventing debris falling or being thrown down the chimney, and ensuring appliances are tested for safety after the work has been completed. (Disconnection/testing of appliances should only be carried out by someone who is, or is employed by, a member of an HSE approved class of persons under regulation 3, eg a Gas Safe-registered engineer.) Similar consideration needs to be given to any proposed alterations which might affect operation of a flue system, eg fitting a flue liner or terminal.

85 In other cases, the effects of the work may not be so obvious. For example, when fitting double glazing or cavity wall insulation, the removal of fixed permanent ventilation, such as air bricks, and replacement with closeable ventilation louvres (in contravention of standards) or blockage of vents by insulation material, can lead to danger from reduced ventilation/incomplete combustion. Equally, fitting extractor fans can lead to the pull on flues being overcome and flue products being sucked back into premises. Moreover, the enclosure of an existing flue terminal within a new extension or conservatory (again in contravention of standards) can lead to flue gases becoming entrapped.

86 Irrespective of how obvious the implications of the work are for gas safety, the people involved need to keep these matters in mind, and ensure they are properly addressed when alterations to premises are planned.

87 Regulation 8(1) applies only to the alteration of premises in which the gas appliance concerned is installed, ie it does not cover any alteration to adjoining premises. Gas appliances/storage vessels should be installed so that safety cannot be affected by any future developments, eg building extensions, on adjoining property. For example, a flue should be located at a safe distance from any site boundary, so that in event of any development on a neighbouring site (which could extend up to the boundary), the flue will continue to operate properly and discharge of combustion products will not present a hazard to any person (see regulation 27 and Appendix 1).

Regulation 8(2)

(2) *No person shall do anything which would affect a gas fitting or any flue or means of ventilation used in connection with the fitting in such a manner that the subsequent use of the fitting might constitute a danger to any person, except that this paragraph does not apply to an alteration to premises.*

Guidance 8(2)

88 This regulation applies to everyone, not just gas engineers. It supplements regulation 8(1), by prohibiting other activities (ie except alteration to premises) which have the potential to compromise safety; this might for instance include modifications which cause blockage/obstruction of an air supply vent or flue, or incorrect installation of an air extraction or condensation control unit. As

with regulation 8(1), it is essential for the implications of any such change or modification to be properly addressed, before work is commenced, to ensure that gas safety cannot be prejudiced in any way.

89 Modification of any gas fitting should be made only by a competent person who is, or is employed by, a member of an HSE approved class of persons (eg Gas Safe registered) under regulation 3(3). Alterations not comprising 'work' on a gas fitting but which nevertheless may affect gas safety, eg a change to room ventilation provisions, should also be made only by a person with the required competence. Similarly, any significant modification needs to be checked by a competent person before the gas fitting concerned is taken into use, to ensure that appropriate standards have been met and safety has not been compromised (see regulation 26(9)).

(3) In relation to any place of work under his control, an employer or a self-employed person shall ensure, so far as is reasonably practicable, that the provisions of paragraphs (1) and (2) are complied with.

90 It is recommended that a responsible person, eg a principal contractor, foreman, site manager or other person with overall control of the work, is nominated to ensure, so far as is reasonably practicable, compliance with regulation 8(1) and (2).

Emergency controls

(1) No person shall for the first time enable gas to be supplied for use in any premises unless there is provided an appropriately sited emergency control to which there is adequate access.

91 A person who allows gas to flow into any premises for the first time should ensure an appropriately sited emergency control is in place.

92 Whenever a new supply of gas is made available for use in premises, an emergency control should also be provided; where there is a gas meter, the meter control may serve as the emergency control as long as the conditions (as follows) are met. Each individual premises (eg each house, flat, maisonette, or caravan) using a supply of gas should be provided with an emergency control, whether or not that premises contains a gas meter. The emergency control should be situated as near as is reasonably practicable to the point where the pipe supplying gas enters the premises. It should be readily assessible to all consumers, ie gas users, in the premises concerned (eg not located in a basement or cellar); therefore, a valve located in a meter-room which is normally locked, and accessible only to a landlord, gas supplier, gas transporter and/or emergency services, for example, cannot act as an 'emergency control'. An emergency control should be protected against unauthorised operation (ie tamper-proof) but if situated in a locked compartment, the occupier(s) of the premises should be provided with keys (see also regulation 13(3)–(4)). In such cases, the emergency service provider should also hold keys where access cannot be ensured for them at all times, eg through keys held by the responsible person for premises.

93 The person allowing the flow of gas to the premises should ensure that every gas consumer in the premises is aware of the location of their emergency control (where there is more than one emergency control, eg in multi-occupancy premises, it is important for the particular control serving that consumer to be identified), and of the action to be taken in case of a gas emergency. In the case of rented property, the responsible person for the building, such as a landlord or managing

Guidance 9(1)

agent, should ensure that all tenants are made aware of this information, including any new tenant moving into property (see also definition of 'emergency control' in regulation 2(2)).

94   Some premises contain separate buildings, eg a domestic property with stables or an office complex with a number of buildings on one site. As long as the premises are clearly under the control of one person or organisation, only one emergency control is required. However, arrangements need to be made in these situations to ensure that the person in control is immediately notified of any gas emergency in the premises, so that suitable action can be taken, eg to isolate the gas supply (see regulation 37).

95   In the case of LPG, this regulation only applies where the gas is supplied from a storage tank or tanks, or from two or more cylinders connected by an automatic changeover device (see regulation 9(5)). In other cases the vapour valve on each cylinder also functions as a shut-off control and no additional provision is necessary.

Regulation 9(2)

(2)   Any person installing an emergency control shall ensure that -

(a)   any key, lever or hand-wheel of the control is securely attached to the operating spindle of the control;
(b)   any such key or lever is attached so that -

(i)   the key or lever is parallel to the axis of the pipe in which the control is installed when the control is in the open position; and
(ii)   where the key or lever is not attached so as to move only horizontally, gas cannot pass beyond the control when the key or lever has been moved as far as possible downwards;

(c)   either the means of operating the key or lever is clearly and permanently marked or a notice in permanent form is prominently displayed near such means so as to indicate when the control is open and when the control is shut; and
(d)   any hand-wheel indicates the direction of opening or closing of the control.

Guidance 9(2)

96   The emergency control can operate by a key, lever or hand-wheel which should be securely attached to the operating spindle of the control. Where a key or lever is used, the 'open' position should be when the key or lever is parallel to the axis of the pipe. The 'off' position should be approximately one quarter turn of the key or lever to the right or left and, where the key or lever moves in the vertical plane, the move to the 'off' position should be in a downwards direction. Either the key or lever itself, or a nearby permanent notice, should indicate how the control operates and when the gas is 'off' and 'on'.

97   Controls operated by hand-wheels need to indicate the opening and/or closing directions for the control.

Regulation 9(3)

(3)   Where a person installs an emergency control which is not adjacent to a primary meter, he shall immediately thereafter prominently display on or near the means of operating the control a suitably worded notice in permanent form indicating the procedure to be followed in the event of an escape of gas.

Guidance 9(3)

98   Where an emergency control is installed which is not adjacent to a primary meter, or where no meter is installed, a prominently displayed notice on or near the control bearing the words 'Gas emergency control' should be provided. The notice needs to tell the consumer:

Guidance
9(3)

(a) to shut off the supply of gas if there is a gas escape in the premises;
(b) if gas continues to escape, immediately notify the Gas Emergency Freephone Number 0800 111 999 (if natural gas). If the gas is not natural gas, notify the supplier emergency service;
(c) not to reinstate the supply until remedial action has been taken by a competent person to prevent gas escaping again;
(d) details of the emergency gas service contact, including the emergency telephone number. In the case of natural gas, the Gas Emergency Freephone Number should be specified (as above); for any other gas, the name and telephone number of the supplier emergency service should be given;
(e) the date the notice was first displayed.

99 The notice should be in a permanent form, ie of durable material, and protected against damage as necessary, eg weather-resistant. See regulation 37 and associated guidance concerning action required in the event of a gas escape.

100 Where an emergency control is installed adjacent to a primary meter, an emergency notice is required to be displayed instead at the meter (see regulation 15).

Regulation 9(4)

(4) Where any person first supplies gas to premises where an emergency control is installed, he shall ensure that the notice required by paragraph (3) above remains suitably worded or shall, where necessary, forthwith amend or replace that notice so as to give effect to the provisions of that paragraph.

Guidance 9(4)

101 If there is a change to the gas supplier which results in a change to the emergency contact point, the notice needs to be updated by the new supplier.

Regulation 9(5)

(5) This regulation shall not apply where gas is supplied in a refillable cylinder except where two or more cylinders are connected by means of an automatic change-over device.

Regulation 10

Maintaining electrical continuity

Regulation 10

In any case where it is necessary to prevent danger, no person shall carry out work in relation to a gas fitting without using a suitable bond to maintain electrical continuity until the work is completed and permanent electrical continuity has been restored.

ACOP 10

102 A temporary continuity bond to the appropriate standard is required when disconnecting and reconnecting pipework where the production of a spark could cause a hazard.

Guidance 10

103 The purpose of the temporary bond is to maintain electrical continuity between the pipework to reduce the risk of a spark causing ignition. Work is not considered to have been completed until the restoration of permanent electrical continuity, where this is necessary to prevent potential hazard. The bond should be fitted with a robust clip or clamp at each end which provides effective electrical contact. See also regulation 18(2) concerning equipotential bonding which addresses the risk of electric shock.

PART C METERS AND REGULATORS

Regulation 11

Regulation

11

Interpretation of Part C

In this Part -

"meter box" means a receptacle or compartment designed and constructed to contain a meter with its associated gas fittings;

"meter compound" means an area or room designed and constructed to contain one or more meters with their associated gas fittings;

"secondary meter" means a meter, other than a primary meter, for ascertaining the quantity of gas provided; by a person for use by another person.

Regulation 12

Regulation

12(1)–(2)

Meters – general provisions

(1) No person shall install a meter in any premises unless the site where it is to be installed is such as to ensure so far as is reasonably practicable that the means of escape from those premises in the event of fire is not adversely affected.

(2) No person shall install a meter in any premises unless it is of sound construction adequate to ensure so far as is reasonably practicable that in the event of fire gas is not able to escape in hazardous quantities, save that this paragraph shall not apply to any meter installed in non-domestic premises to which gas is supplied through a readily accessible service valve.

ACOP

12(1)–(2)

104 Before any meter is installed, a check should be made on the means of escape from the premises in the event of fire. Meters and meter compartments, and their installation, need to conform to the appropriate standard.

Guidance

General

105 Building designers and contractors need to consult the gas supplier/transporter mutually to agree the position and housing for primary meters at an early stage in any new building development.

New installations (premises with two or more floors above the ground floor)

106 Meters should not be sited on or under the stairway, or in any other part of the premises, where the stairway or that other part of the premises forms the sole means of escape in case of fire.

All other installations (including premises with less than two floors above the ground floor and replacement meters in premises with two or more floors above the ground floor)

107 Meters need to be installed, where reasonably practicable, in accordance with paragraph 106. If it is necessary to install a new or replacement meter on or under a stairway, or in any other part of premises, where the stairway or that other part of the premises forms the sole means of escape in the case of fire:

12(1)–(2)

(a) the meter should be fire-resistant; or

Guidance

12(1)–(2)

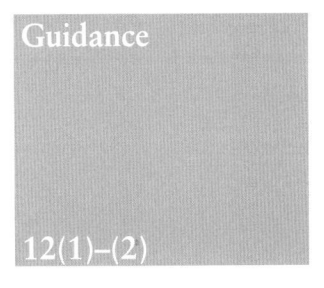

(b) the meter should be housed in a fire-resistant compartment with automatic self-closing doors; or
(c) the pipe immediately upstream of the meter, or regulator if fitted, should be provided with a thermal cut-off device which is designed to automatically cut off the gas supply if the temperature of the device exceeds 95°C.

108 Due account should be taken of relevant requirements in the Building Regulations. It may be necessary to install meters in meter rooms or compounds.

Regulation 12(3)

(3) *No person shall install a meter unless the installation is so placed as to ensure that there is no risk of damage to it from electrical apparatus.*

ACOP 12(3)

109 Before installing a meter, checks should be made on the location and type of any electrical apparatus in the vicinity. Separation distances between gas meter installations and electrical apparatus are specified in the appropriate standards.

Regulation

(4) *No person shall install a meter except in a readily accessible position for inspection and maintenance.*

(5) *Where a meter has bosses or side pipes attached to the meter by a soldered joint only, no person shall make rigid pipe connections to the meter.*

(6) *Where a person installs a meter and the pipes and other gas fittings associated with it, he shall ensure that -*

(a) *immediately thereafter they are adequately tested to verify that they are gas tight and examined to verify that they have been installed in accordance with these Regulations; and*
(b) *immediately after such testing and examination, purging is carried out throughout the meter and every other gas fitting through which gas can then flow so as to remove safely all air and gas other than the gas to be supplied.*

12(4)–(6)

ACOP 12(4)–(6)

110 The connections should be tested for gastightness in accordance with the appropriate standard. The whole installation should then be purged including any appliances connected to the system, again in accordance with the appropriate standard.

Regulation 13

Meter housings

Regulation 13(1)–(2)

(1) *Where a meter is housed in a meter box or meter compound attached to or built into the external face of the outside wall of any premises, the meter box or meter compound shall be so constructed and installed that any gas escaping within the box or compound cannot enter the premises or any cavity in the wall but must disperse to the external air.*

(2) *No person shall knowingly store readily combustible materials in any meter box or meter compound.*

Guidance 13(1)–(2)

111 Potential routes for gas leakage from a meter box or compound into a premises or wall cavity should be effectively sealed. Particular care needs to be taken adequately to sleeve and seal around an installation pipe where it passes from the meter box and enters a building, eg via a cavity (see also regulation 19).

112 Regulation 13(2) applies to everyone, not just gas installers. Meter boxes or compounds should not, for example, be used for storage of combustible household waste such as paper and cardboard.

Regulation 13(3)–(4)

(3) No person shall install a meter in a meter box provided with a lock, unless the consumer has been provided with a suitably labelled key to that lock.

(4) No person shall install a meter within a meter compound which is capable of being secured unless the consumer has been provided with a suitably labelled key for that compound.

Regulation 14

Regulators

Regulation 14(1)

(1) No person shall install a primary meter or meter by pass used in connection with a primary meter unless -

(a) there is a regulator controlling the pressure of gas supplied through the meter or the by pass, as the case may be, which provides adequate automatic means for preventing the gas fittings connected to the downstream side of the regulator from being subjected to a pressure greater than that for which they were designed;

(b) where the normal pressure of the gas supply is 75 millibars or more at the inlet to the regulator, there are also adequate automatic means for preventing, in case the regulator should fail, those gas fittings from being subjected to such a greater pressure; and

(c) where the regulator contains a relief valve or liquid seal, such valve or seal is connected to a vent pipe of adequate size and so installed that it is capable of venting safely.

Guidance 14(1)

113 An overpressure shut-off device or pressure relief valve may be used to prevent exposure of downstream fittings to excessive pressure in event of regulator failure. Requirements for protection against overpressure in the case of gas (eg LPG) installations supplied from vessels or cylinders are given in regulation 14(2)–(4).

114 Any vent pipe should discharge to open air rather than into any part of a building, and should terminate away from potential ignition sources. Reference should be made to appropriate standards.

Regulation 14(2)

(2) Without prejudice to the requirements of paragraph (1), no person shall cause gas to be supplied from a gas storage vessel (other than a re-fillable cylinder or a cylinder or cartridge designed to be disposed of when empty) to any service pipework or gas fitting unless -

(a) there is a regulator installed which controls the nominal operating pressure of the gas;

(b) there is adequate automatic means for preventing the installation pipework and gas fittings downstream of the regulator from being subjected to a pressure different from that for which they were designed; and

(c) there is an adequate alternative automatic means for preventing the service pipework from being subjected to a greater pressure than that for which it was designed should the regulator referred to in sub-paragraph (a) above fail.

Guidance 14(2)

115 Regulation 14(2) applies only to installations using gas (essentially LPG) stored in bulk vessels or tanks. Any such installation should be provided with:

(a) a regulator to maintain the gas supply pressure within the range at which appliances downstream were designed to operate safely; and

Guidance

14(2)

(b) an overpressure and underpressure shut-off device (OPSO/UPSO), to provide back-up protection if the regulator fails or the gas supply pressure falls to a dangerously low level, eg because the storage vessel has become empty.

In addition, where there is a risk of service pipework failing if the regulator malfunctions, the pipework should be protected by a further overpressure shut-off device to prevent such failure. This is normally required only for non-metallic pipework.

116 Installed pressure systems and associated gas storage vessels should comply with the Pressure Systems Safety Regulations 2000, where applicable (see Appendix 3). Any regulator, over- or underpressure protection device required under regulation 14(1)–(4) should be designed, constructed and installed in accordance with the appropriate standards.

Regulation

14(3)–(4)

(3) No person shall cause gas to be supplied through an installation consisting of one or more re-fillable cylinders unless the supply of gas passes through a regulator which controls the nominal operating pressure of the gas.

(4) Without prejudice to paragraph (3) above, no person shall cause gas to be supplied through an installation consisting of four or more re-fillable cylinders connected to an automatic change-over device unless there is an adequate alternative means for preventing the installation pipework and any gas fitting downstream of the regulator from being subjected to a greater pressure than that for which it was designed should the regulator fail.

Guidance

14(3)–(4)

117 Regulation 14(3)–(4) applies only to installations using gas (ie essentially LPG) from cylinders. As with installations using bulk vessels, a regulator should be provided to protect appliances downstream from being subjected to a pressure outside their safe operating range. If the cylinder supply comprises four or more cylinders connected to an automatic changeover device, an overpressure protection device should, in addition, be fitted to prevent downstream appliances, and pipework, being subjected to a pressure above that for which they were designed, should the regulator fail. Automatic cylinder changeover devices should comply with the appropriate standard.

Regulation

14(5)–(7)

(5) Where a person installs a regulator for controlling the pressure of gas through a primary meter, a meter by pass used in connection with a primary meter or from a gas storage vessel, or installs a gas appliance itself fitted with a regulator for controlling the pressure of gas to that appliance, he shall immediately thereafter ensure, in either case, that the regulator is adequately sealed so as to prevent its setting from being interfered with without breaking of the seal.

(6) In relation to -

(a) gas from a distribution main, no person except the transporter or a person authorised to act on his behalf;
(b) gas from a gas storage vessel, no person except the supplier or a person authorised to act on his behalf,

shall break a seal applied under paragraph (5) above other than a seal applied to a regulator for controlling the pressure of gas to the appliance to which that regulator is fitted.

(7) A person who breaks a seal applied under paragraph (5) shall apply as soon as is practicable a new seal which is adequate to prevent the setting of the regulator from being interfered with without breaking such seal.

Guidance

14(5)–(7)

118 Regulation 14(6) generally restricts the breaking of regulator seals to the gas transporter or supplier in the particular situation, or someone authorised to act on their behalf. However, a competent person may adjust a regulator on an individual appliance, eg to check the correct operating pressure, without the need for authorisation to break the seal.

119 Any person who breaks a seal should ensure that it is replaced with a suitable equivalent seal, as soon as the work has been completed.

Regulation 15

Meters – emergency notices

Regulation

15(1)–(2)

(1) No person shall supply gas through a primary meter installed after the coming into force of these Regulations or for the first time supply gas through an existing primary meter after the coming into force of these Regulations unless he ensures that a suitably worded notice in permanent form is prominently displayed on or near the meter indicating the procedure to be followed in the event of an escape of gas.

(2) Where a meter is installed or relocated in any premises in either case at a distance of more than 2 metres from, or out of sight of, the nearest upstream emergency control in the premises, no person shall supply or provide gas for the first time through that meter unless he ensures that a suitably worded notice in permanent form is prominently displayed on or near the meter indicating the position of that control.

ACOP

15(1)–(2)

120 Any supplier of gas through a primary meter should ensure that the required emergency notice is in place. Where there is a change in gas supplier which involves a change in the emergency service provider, the notice will need to be updated/replaced to reflect such a change.

Guidance

121 Whenever a primary meter is installed in premises, an emergency notice is required to be prominently displayed on or near the meter. The notice should contain the information for the gas consumer, as specified in paragraph 98(a)–(e).

122 If the nearest upstream emergency control is installed in or subsequently relocated to a position out of sight of the meter or, in any case, in a position more than 2 metres away from the meter, a notice should be displayed on or near the meter concerned, indicating the position of the emergency control.

123 Notices required under regulation 15 should be in a permanent form, ie of durable material, and protected against damage as necessary, eg weather-resistant. The notice(s) should not obscure other information shown on a meter. See regulation 37 and associated guidance concerning action required in the event of a gas escape.

124 Where an emergency control is not located adjacent to a primary meter, an emergency notice is required instead to be displayed on or near to the emergency control (see regulation 9(3)).

15(1)–(2)

Regulation 16

Primary meters

Regulation
16(1)–(2)

(1) No person shall install a prepayment meter as a primary meter through which gas passes to a secondary meter.

Regulation

16(1)–(2)

(2) Any person -

(a) who first provides gas through any service pipe or service pipework after the coming into force of these Regulations to more than one primary meter; or
(b) who subsequently makes any modification which affects the number of primary meters so provided,

shall ensure that a notice in permanent form is prominently displayed on or near each primary meter indicating that more than one primary meter is provided with gas through that service pipe or service pipework.

Guidance

16(1)–(2)

125 Regulation 16(1) prohibits the use of a prepayment meter as a primary meter, where gas is passed on to a secondary meter(s), because use of such a meter would (when money runs out) cause the gas supply to all consumers on the system to be immediately cut off. This would lead to a potential risk of gas escape where any gas appliance has not been isolated before the gas supply is resumed, eg because the user is away at the time (see also paragraph 131).

126 The purpose of the notice required under regulation 16(2) is to make gas engineers, emergency services etc aware of the possible implications for other users, eg if the gas supply needs to be isolated. The notice is required both for new installations and where an existing system is modified so that more than one primary meter is then supplied from a service pipe or service pipework; in the case of modifications, the person making the change is responsible for ensuring the notice is displayed. It is recommended that the notice also indicates the number and location of other meters supplied from the same service pipe or pipework, and that any person who carries out an alteration affecting the accuracy of the information provided should ensure that the notice is amended accordingly.

Regulation

16(3)–(4)

(3) *Where a primary meter is removed, the person who last supplied gas through the meter before removal shall -*

(a) *where the meter is not forthwith re-installed or replaced by another meter -*

(i) *close any service valve which controlled the supply of gas to that meter and did not control the supply of gas to any other primary meter; and*
(ii) *seal the outlet of the emergency control with an appropriate fitting; and*
(iii) *clearly mark any live gas pipe in the premises in which the meter was installed to the effect that the pipe contains gas; and*

(b) *where the meter has not been re-installed or replaced by another meter before the expiry of the period of 12 months beginning with the date of removal of the meter and there is no such service valve as is mentioned in sub-paragraph (a)(i) above, ensure that the service pipe or service pipework for those premises is disconnected as near as is reasonably practicable to the main or storage vessel and that any part of the pipe or pipework which is not removed is sealed at both ends with the appropriate fitting.*

(4) *Where a person proposes to remove a primary meter he shall give sufficient notice of it to the person supplying gas through the meter to enable him to comply with paragraph (3).*

Guidance

127 Regulation 16(3)(b) interfaces with the duty on pipeline operators under the Pipelines Safety Regulations 1996 (PSR) to ensure that certain disused pipelines are left in a safe condition; further information is given in the ACOP *Design, construction and installation of gas service pipes* (see Appendices 3 and 4). In the case of any gas service pipe (covered by PSR), the supplier needs to ensure, so far as is reasonably practicable, that the action stipulated in regulation 16(3)(b) is taken by the public gas transporter (ie the dutyholder under PSR). In the case of pipework not covered by PSR, eg an LPG system on a caravan or mobile home site, the 'gas supplier' will need to take the necessary action to disconnect/seal pipework or make appropriate arrangements for this to be done by, eg a suitable contractor; in either case the work should be carried out only by a person meeting the requirements of regulation 3. See definition of 'supplier' in regulation 2(1) and associated guidance concerning allocation of duties in particular circumstances.

128 Regulation 16(3)(b) requires disconnection 'as near as is reasonably practicable' to the main or storage tank, providing flexibility to cover circumstances where disconnection at the main or storage tank itself might be very difficult. The regulation also recognises certain situations, eg blocks of flats, where removal of service pipes or service pipework to particular dwellings may not be readily achievable. The gas supplier (together with the transporter in the case of natural gas) needs to decide the appropriate action in a particular case, bearing in mind that unused 'live' service pipes or pipework represent a potential hazard. Metal fittings should be used to seal metal pipes (and outlets of emergency controls under regulation 16(3)(a)), see also definition of 'appropriate fitting' in regulation 2(1). It should also be ensured that any installation pipework or other gas fitting rendered redundant by meter removal is made safe (eg by purging, and sealing any open gasways with an appropriate fitting).

129 Regulation 16(4) recognises that meters may be removed by persons other than gas suppliers. Close co-operation with the 'last supplier' of gas is essential in these circumstances, and sufficient notice of any proposed meter removal should be given to enable the supplier to take effective action under regulation 16(3).

16(3)–(4)

Regulation 17

Secondary meters

Regulation

(1) Any person supplying or permitting the supply of gas through a primary meter to a secondary meter shall ensure that a line diagram in permanent form is prominently displayed on or near the primary meter or gas storage vessel and on or near all emergency controls connected to the primary meter showing the configuration of all meters, installation pipework and emergency controls.

(2) Any person who changes the configuration of any meter, installation pipework or emergency control so that the accuracy of the line diagram referred to in paragraph (1) is affected shall ensure that the line diagram is amended so as to show the altered configuration.

17(1)–(2)

Guidance

130 Where a gas supply is provided through a primary meter to secondary meter(s), ie to a number of downstream consumers, the information required by this regulation is important for several reasons. For example, in the case of a flat or house in multiple occupation, an engineer or the emergency services would require information on the location/configuration of emergency control valves and pipework to isolate the gas supply to a particular dwelling; and to establish how this would affect the supply to other consumers in the premises. Similarly, this information would be required when supplies to individual consumers needed to be checked, eg after disconnection or reconnection of pipework.

17(1)–(2)

Guidance

17(1)–(2)

131 The situation may be further complicated in 'sub-deduct' situations, ie where secondary meters are used by one or more gas supplier(s) for establishing charges to downstream consumers, by a process of deduction from the total quantity of gas supplied through a primary meter (see Gas Act 1995 – Network Code, section G1). In such cases, a configuration may be complex, involving several sub-deduct meters, associated pipework and emergency controls, together with the primary meter. The availability of clear and unambiguous information on these configurations is essential, for instance, to avoid situations where action to isolate the supply to one consumer unknowingly interrupts someone else's supply (leading to possible risk of a gas escape where appliances are not isolated before the supply is reinstated, eg because the user is away at the time).

132 The notice is required to contain the information specified in regulation 15(1); a diagram showing the configuration in outline will normally be sufficient for this purpose, ie a detailed scale plan is not necessary. The diagram should be displayed in a prominent position at the primary meter (or gas storage vessel if the gas is so supplied) and at all emergency controls connected to the primary meter, in the premises. The duty to provide the notice(s) rests with the person supplying or permitting the supply of gas through the primary meter. This might be a gas supplier (eg in sub-deduct situations) or a landlord providing gas to a tenant. Where there is more than one dutyholder, effective liaison is essential to ensure requirements are met.

133 Regulation 17(2) requires any person making a change to the configuration of any installation pipework, meter, or emergency control to ensure the notice originally provided under regulation 17(1) is suitably amended, where this is necessary to preserve accuracy for safety purposes, as described in paragraphs 130–131. The notice is not required to be modified in respect of minor changes which do not have implications for safety identification purposes, eg where there is a small change in location of a relevant fitting but relative positions are unaffected.

134 The advice of a competent gas engineer needs to be sought on the wording of the notice. In addition to the information specified in regulation 17, it is recommended that notices indicate the person responsible for each section of installation in the premises. The notice may be based on the system diagram required under regulation 24, where applicable.

PART D INSTALLATION PIPEWORK

Regulation 18

Safe use of pipes

Regulation

18(1)–(2)

(1) *No person shall install any installation pipework in any position in which it cannot be used with safety having regard to the position of other pipes, pipe supports, drains, sewers, cables, conduits and electrical apparatus and to any parts of the structure of any premises in which it is installed which might affect its safe use.*

(2) *Any person who connects any installation pipework to a primary meter shall, in any case where equipotential bonding may be necessary, inform the responsible person that such bonding should be carried out by a competent person.*

ACOP

18(1)–(2)

135 The location and routing of installation pipework should take into account the potential risk, eg of corrosion damage, posed by the other building services, equipment and features specified in regulation 18(1), for instance by providing adequate separation. Pipework installation and equipotential bonding should be carried out to the appropriate standard.

Guidance

136 Main equipotential bonding (sometimes known as 'electrical cross bonding') is the connection between the consumer earth point and the gas installation pipe. The purpose is to create a zone (eg within a dwelling), including the area occupied by the gas installation pipework, within which acceptable voltage differences are maintained, in order to avoid the risk of electric shock. Such bonding does not involve connecting electrical power to gas pipes.

137 The regulation places an obligation upon the person who installs a section of pipework which connects with the primary meter or emergency control, whether or not the meter or control has yet been fitted, to inform the responsible person for the premises (builder, owner or occupier) of the possible need for main equipotential bonding where such a requirement did not exist before the work was undertaken, and that such bonding should be carried out by a competent person. The advice should be in writing. Although the regulation applies only when new systems are installed and existing ones are modified, similar action needs to be taken if an engineer notices an apparent defect in bonding in other circumstances, eg during maintenance checks (this applies to both main or supplementary equipotential bonding – see also paragraph 141 below).

138 Main equipotential bonding is most commonly required where:

(a) gas pipework is installed in new premises; or
(b) gas pipework is first installed in existing premises.

139 The regulation is directed at the 600 mm (approximate) length of installation pipework at the outlet of the domestic meter installation which is the recommended location of any main equipotential bond in the appropriate standard.

140 The requirements for main equipotential bonding are more strict for certain types of electrical supply to premises (eg those supplies from protective multiple earth (PME) systems – most new electrical supplies will be from such systems). A gas engineer may not be competent to make the necessary judgement, in which case the responsible person needs to be informed of this fact and any further action left to them.

18(1)–(2)

Guidance 18(1)–(2)

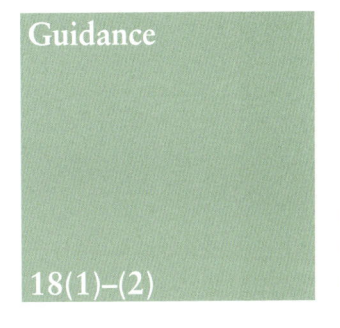

141 Regulation 18(2) does not apply to the installation of a meter. In addition to main bonding, supplementary equipotential bonding of pipework may be necessary in locations of increased electric shock risk, eg bathrooms. In such cases, a competent electrical engineer should be consulted.

142 In many commercial and other large sites where gas and electric meters may be remotely located, the bonding is not always possible within a 600 mm distance. A competent electrical engineer needs to consider what action is necessary in these cases.

Regulation 19

Enclosed pipes

Regulation 19(1)

(1) No person shall install any part of any installation pipework in a wall or a floor or standing of solid construction unless it is so constructed and installed as to be protected against failure caused by the movement of the wall, the floor or the standing as the case may be.

Guidance 19(1)

143 The appropriate standard describes suitable installation methods.

Regulation 19(2)–(6)

(2) No person shall install any installation pipework so as to pass through a wall or a floor or standing of solid construction (whether or not it contains any cavity) from one side to the other unless -

(a) any part of the pipe within such wall, floor or standing as the case may be takes the shortest practicable route; and
(b) adequate means are provided to prevent, so far as is reasonably practicable, any escape of gas from the pipework passing through the wall, floor or standing from entering any cavity in the wall, floor or standing.

(3) No person shall, subject to paragraph 4, install any part of any installation pipework in the cavity of a cavity wall unless the pipe is to pass through the wall from one side to the other.

(4) Paragraph (3) shall not apply to the installation of installation pipework connected to a living flame effect fire provided that the pipework in the cavity is as short as is reasonably practicable, is enclosed in a gas tight sleeve and sealed at the joint at which the pipework enters the fire; and in this paragraph a "living flame effect gas fire" means a gas fire -

(a) designed to simulate the effect of a solid fuel fire;
(b) designed to operate with a fanned flue system; and
(c) installed within the inner leaf of a cavity wall.

(5) No person shall install any installation pipework or any service pipework under the foundations of a building or in the ground under the base of a wall or footings unless adequate steps are taken to prevent damage to the installation pipework or service pipework in the event of the movement of those structures or the ground.

(6) Where any installation pipework is not itself contained in a ventilated duct, no person shall install any installation pipework in any shaft, duct or void which is not adequately ventilated.

Guidance

19(2)–(6)

144 Regulation 19(2)(b) addresses the potential risk of gas leaking from pipework within a cavity in a wall, floor or standing; such leakage may be difficult to detect and readily lead to the accumulation of an explosive gas/air mixture in the cavity, presenting a considerable hazard to building occupants and others. The protective measures required may include enclosing that part of the pipe which passes through the wall, floor or standing in a gastight sleeve which itself is ventilated to a safe position, preferably to open air. This approach also provides some protection against possible mechanical damage to pipework, arising from structural movement (see also regulation 19(5)); any gap between the pipe and sleeve should be sealed (with flexible sealant), but at one end only so as to ensure any leak cannot accumulate in the gap space.

145 Shafts, ducts and voids used for accommodation of gas pipework should comply with the appropriate standard. It should be ensured that measures to comply with regulation 19, eg void/duct ventilation arrangements, do not impair any provisions for fire/smoke separation in a building – see regulation 20.

146 The exception for 'living flame effect' fires in regulation 19(4) applies only to those fires of this type which operate with a fanned flue system (ie where removal of combustion products depends on a fan rather than natural draught through a flue/chimney) and are installed within the inner leaf of a cavity wall. Although pipework connected to these fires may be 'hidden' by routing within a cavity, without the restriction in regulation 19(3), the length of pipework in the cavity is still required to be kept as short as is reasonably practicable, ie by taking the most direct route consistent with requirements for the particular installation. The installation of 'living flame effect' fires and associated flue systems, as covered by regulation 19(4), normally involves work which may affect the structural integrity of a building; requirements of Building Regulations should be met, as appropriate.

Regulation 20

Regulation 20

Protection of buildings

No person shall install any installation pipework in a way which would impair the structure of a building or impair the fire resistance of any part of its structure.

Regulation 21

Regulation 21

Clogging precautions

No person shall install any installation pipework in which deposition of liquid or solid matter is likely to occur unless a suitable vessel for the reception of any deposit which may form is fixed to the pipe in a conspicuous and readily accessible position and safe means are provided for the removal of the deposit.

Guidance 21

147 Natural gas and LPG are 'dry' gases and do not normally require such fittings. Engineers working with gases which might cause solid or liquid deposits (eg gas produced from landfill or by anaerobic digestion in certain circumstances) should refer to the appropriate standard.

Regulation 22

Regulation 22(1)

Testing and purging of pipes

(1) Where a person carries out work in relation to any installation pipework which might affect the gastightness of any part of it, he shall immediately thereafter ensure that -

(a) that part is adequately tested to verify that it is gastight and examined to verify that it has been installed in accordance with these Regulations; and

ACOP 22(1)

148 Gastightness requirements are set out in the appropriate standard. All joints affected by the portion of work done should be visually inspected to ensure they have been correctly made, as part of the gastightness test.

Regulation 22(1)

(b) after such testing and examination, any necessary protective coating is applied to the joints of that part.

ACOP 22(1)

149 Joints should be tested before being painted or otherwise protected against corrosion.

Guidance 22(1)

150 Painting a joint before it has been tested could provide a temporary seal, and falsify the test result.

Regulation 22(2)

(2) Where gas is being supplied to any premises in which any installation pipework is installed and a person carries out work in relation to the pipework, he shall also ensure that -

(a) immediately after complying with the provisions of sub-paragraphs (a) and (b) of paragraph (1) above, purging is carried out throughout all installation pipework through which gas can then flow so as to remove safely all air and gas other than the gas to be supplied;

(b) immediately after such purging, if the pipework is not to be put into immediate use, it is sealed off at every outlet with the appropriate fitting;

(c) if such purging has been carried out through a loosened connection, the connection is retested for gastightness after it has been retightened; and

(d) every seal fitted after such purging is tested for gastightness.

ACOP 22(2)

151 Purging should be carried out in accordance with the appropriate standard and should be undertaken after any work which breaches the integrity of installation pipework, not just when gas is first supplied. Requirements in relation to an 'appropriate fitting' are given under the definition in regulation 2(1).

Regulation 22(3)

(3) Where gas is not being supplied to any premises in which any installation pipework is installed -

(a) no person shall permit gas to pass into the installation pipework unless he has caused such purging, testing and other work as is specified in sub-paragraphs (a) to (d) of paragraph (2) above to be carried out;

(b) a person who provides a gas supply to those premises shall, unless he complies with sub-paragraph (a) above, ensure that the supply is sealed off with an appropriate fitting.

Guidance 22(3)

152 This regulation applies when a premises is first being supplied with gas. It does not apply where gas has been temporarily cut off, eg where an emergency control has been shut off, or an over/under pressure valve has operated. Neither does it apply to situations merely involving a change in supplier of gas to a premises.

153 In some cases, a gas supply may be provided some time before installation work is done, or vice versa. Where this occurs, the supply or installation pipework should be properly capped so that no third party, eg the occupant, can easily interfere with it. The person finally connecting the supply to the installation is responsible for testing and purging the pipe system in accordance with regulation 22(2).

Regulation 23

Regulation 23(1)

Marking of pipes

(1) Any person installing, elsewhere than in any premises or part of premises used only as a dwelling or for living accommodation, a part of any installation pipework which is accessible to inspection shall permanently mark that part in such a manner that it is readily recognisable as part of a pipe for conveying gas.

Guidance 23(1)

154 This regulation does not apply to domestic premises or living accommodation. In all other locations, eg commercial premises such as offices, gas pipes accessible to inspection should be colour coded and/or marked in accordance with the appropriate standard.

Regulation 23(2)

(2) The responsible person for the premises in which any such part is situated shall ensure that the part continues to be so recognisable so long as it is used for conveying gas.

Regulation 24

Regulation 24(1)–(3)

Large consumers

(1) Where the service pipe to any building having two or more floors to which gas is supplied or (whether or not it has more than one floor) a floor having areas with a separate supply of gas has an internal diameter of 50 mm or more, no person shall install any incoming installation pipework supplying gas to any of those floors or areas, as the case may be, unless -

(a) a valve is installed in the pipe in a conspicuous and readily accessible position; and
(b) a line diagram in permanent form is attached to the building in a readily accessible position as near as practicable to -

(i) the primary meter or where there is no primary meter, the emergency control, or
(ii) the gas storage vessel, indicating the position of all installation pipework of internal diameter of 25 mm or more, meters, emergency controls, valves and pressure test points of the gas supply systems in the building.

(2) Paragraph (1) above shall apply to service pipework as it applies to a service pipe except that reference therein to "50 mm or more" is to be reference to "30 mm or more".

(3) In paragraph (1)(b) above "pressure test point" means a gas fitting to which a pressure gauge can be connected.

Guidance 24(1)–(3)

155 This regulation applies where a service pipe has an internal diameter of 50 mm or more, or service pipework has an internal diameter of 30 mm or more, and divides to supply more than one floor, or separate areas on one floor. This situation is most often encountered in industrial and commercial premises.

156 Where, in order to comply with regulation 24(1)(a), an isolation valve needs to be installed in the service pipe, it is essential to notify the gas transporter and make necessary arrangements, eg for isolation and degassing as necessary, in order to ensure this can be done safely. The system diagram should be prominently displayed at or near to the primary meter or if there is no such meter, the emergency control; where gas is supplied from a storage vessel, the notice may alternatively be displayed at or near to that vessel. Depending on the

Guidance

24(1)–(3)

size of the premises, other copies may be held elsewhere, eg the security gate or reception area.

157 The purpose of the system diagram is to allow anyone, especially the emergency services, to identify and isolate part of the gas system if necessary. Pipes of less than 25 mm do not need to be shown on the diagram but it is recommended that information in addition to that specified in regulation 24(1)(a) be included, where considered significant in respect of the safety of a particular installation, eg this might include purge connections. The diagram needs to be updated as necessary.

PART E GAS APPLIANCES

Regulation 25

Regulation 25

Interpretation of Part E

In this Part -

"flue pipe" means a pipe forming a flue but does not include a pipe built as a lining into either a chimney or a gas appliance ventilation duct;

"operating pressure", in relation to a gas appliance, means the pressure of gas at which it is designed to operate.

Regulation 26

Regulation 26(1)

Gas appliances – safety precautions

(1) No person shall install a gas appliance unless it can be used without constituting a danger to any person.

ACOP 26(1)

158 Gas installers should ensure that any appliance they install, or flue to which they connect an appliance, is safe for use. Requirements in Appendix 1 should be met, as applicable, and reference made to appropriate standards.

159 Appliances should be installed in accordance with the manufacturer's instructions, including any on flues to which they can be safely connected.

Guidance 26(1)

160 This regulation imposes an important and wide-ranging duty on the engineer to ensure that nothing about an appliance itself, the manner in which it is installed, any associated fitting or flue, or other factor (eg ventilation) will cause danger when the appliance is taken into use. This 'all-embracing' duty interfaces with other parts of GSIUR dealing with more specific safety aspects of appliance installation, and requirements under regulation 26(9) for examination/testing after any work on an appliance, including installation. Regulation 30 places restrictions/ prohibitions on the installation of certain appliances; without prejudice to those controls, the installation of an open-flued appliance in the same room (this includes a through lounge) as a solid fuel open fire, or an appliance with a fan-assisted flue, is not recommended (see appropriate standards in Appendix 4).

Regulation 26(2)

(2) No person shall connect a flued domestic gas appliance to the gas supply system except by a permanently fixed rigid pipe.

Guidance 26(2)

161 Flexible connections should not be used as this could allow consumers to move the appliance away from the flue. See also regulation 5(2) concerning construction materials for pipes and pipe fittings.

Regulation 26(3)

(3) No person shall install a used gas appliance without verifying that it is in a safe condition for further use.

Guidance 26(3)

162 Regulation 26(3) requires the physical condition of any used appliance to be checked before installation. This is necessary as suitable inspection might not be possible after an appliance has been installed.

163 In addition to second-hand appliances, this regulation also applies when an appliance is moved from one location to another, even within the same room.

Regulation 26(4)

(4) *No person shall install a gas appliance which does not comply with any enactment imposing a prohibition or restriction on the supply of such an appliance on grounds of safety.*

Guidance 26(4)

164 New appliances should conform to the Gas Appliances (Safety) Regulations 1995 (see Appendix 3).

Regulation 26(5)

(5) *No person carrying out the installation of a gas appliance shall leave it connected to the gas supply unless -*

(a) *the appliance can be used safely; or*
(b) *the appliance is sealed off from the gas supply with an appropriate fitting.*

Guidance 26(5)

165 An appliance should be properly commissioned and checked for safe operation immediately after it has been installed and connected to the gas supply (see also regulation 33). If this cannot be done, the appliance should be sealed off from the gas supply by capping off the installation pipework serving the appliance, using an appropriate fitting. For requirements concerning an 'appropriate fitting' see definition in regulation 2(1) and associated guidance.

Regulation 26(6)

(6) *No person shall install a gas appliance without there being at the inlet to it means of shutting off the supply of gas to the appliance unless the provision of such means is not reasonably practicable.*

Guidance 26(6)

166 The means of shutting off the gas supply to an appliance may comprise either a conventional isolation valve, or other effective means, eg a self-sealing plug-in connector (commonly used on cooker installations) or a screw down restrictor elbow (such as used on gas fire installations). A shut-off device at the inlet to a gas appliance is regarded as part of 'installation pipework' for the purpose of these Regulations (see definition in regulation 2(1)).

167 The shut-off device required under this regulation not only assists soundness testing of installation pipework (see paragraph 70) but also allows an appliance to be isolated/disconnected in case of an emergency, eg if the appliance develops a gas leak or otherwise becomes dangerous. Although the regulation recognises that provision of a shut-off device at the inlet of an appliance might occasionally be difficult, there will be few, if any, situations where this is not reasonably practicable.

Regulation 26(7)–(10)

(7) *No person shall carry out any work in relation to a gas appliance which bears an indication that it conforms to a type approved by any person as complying with safety standards in such a manner that the appliance ceases to comply with those standards.*

(8) *No person carrying out work in relation to a gas appliance which bears an indication that it so conforms shall remove or deface the indication.*

(9) *Where a person performs work on a gas appliance he shall immediately thereafter examine -*

(a) *the effectiveness of any flue;*
(b) *the supply of combustion air;*
(c) *its operating pressure or heat input or, where necessary, both;*
(d) *its operation so as to ensure its safe functioning,*

and forthwith take all reasonably practicable steps to notify any defect to the responsible person and, where different, the owner of the premises in which the

Regulation

26(7)–(10)

appliance is situated or, where neither is reasonably practicable, in the case of an appliance supplied with liquefied petroleum gas, the supplier of gas to the appliance, or, in any other case, the transporter.

(10) Paragraph 9 shall not apply in respect of -

(a) the direct disconnection of the gas supply of a gas appliance; or
(b) the purging of gas or air from an appliance or its associated pipework or fittings in any case where that purging does not adversely affect the safety of that appliance, pipe or fitting.

ACOP

26(7)–(10)

168 After performing work on an installed appliance, installers should carry out the necessary checks and tests to ensure that the appliance, and any associated flue, is safe for use. Requirements in Appendix 1 should be met, as applicable, and reference made to appropriate standards.

Guidance

169 Nothing should be done to a gas appliance which will result in it no longer complying with the standard(s) to which it purports to comply, ie as required by the conformity (eg 'CE') marking on the appliance. Any repair to a gas appliance, for instance involving use of refurbished or reconditioned parts, should be done in a way which ensures safety standards are maintained. Engineers should refer to manufacturer specifications/instructions and appropriate standards.

170 Regulation 26(9) requires a check to be made to ensure that the operating (ie gas) pressure and/or heat input of the appliance is correct. The engineer should carry out the most appropriate test(s) for the appliance. This information is usually shown in manufacturer installation instructions, or on the appliance data badge. In certain cases, eg when appliance burners are modified or replaced, such as for conversion from LPG to natural gas, it may be necessary to check both operating pressure and heat input.

171 Regulation 26(9) applies only to work on gas appliances, it does not cover work on certain other gas fittings, eg meters and installation pipework (that might be carried out remote from an appliance) – see definitions of 'gas appliance' and 'gas fittings' in regulation 2(1). However, appropriate checks and tests are still required to ensure safety after any work has been done on such fittings, eg see regulations 6(6), 12(6) and 22(1). See also exceptions in regulation 2(6)(c) for work on certain gas appliance control devices primarily intended for use by the consumer.

172 Under regulation 26(10), the tests/examinations in regulation 26(9) are not required after certain work on appliances. The exception applies, for instance, to the direct disconnection of an appliance, ie where the appliance is itself detached from the gas supply, such as at the appliance connector or a nearby pipework connection. (Indirect disconnection, eg resulting from removal of another fitting upstream, such as a meter, is separately excluded as this is not regarded as work on a gas appliance – see paragraph 171.)

173 Regulation 26(9) also does not apply in respect of the purging of air or gas from an appliance, eg in the process of resuming a gas supply after interruption, but this is conditional on the purging operation itself having no adverse affect on the safety of any gas fitting. (This would not preclude the possibility of an appliance defect present before, and completely unrelated to, the purging activity still remaining after purging has been completed; such defects would need to be detected and addressed separately, eg see regulations 35 and 36.) In order to establish whether the safety of any gas fitting might be affected by purging, an assessment should be made by a competent person before the operation is carried out; in any case of doubt or where safety is likely to be affected, the

26(7)–(10)

Guidance

26(7)–(10)

tests/examinations in regulation 26(9) should be carried out after purging has been completed, and remedial action taken to make appliances/fittings safe, as necessary.

174 It should be stressed that the exceptions in regulation 26(10) apply only to those activities specifically mentioned and if other work is carried out in association with these activities, eg any adjustment of appliances after purging, the requirements in regulation 26(9) again need to be met.

175 Engineers need to take account of manufacturer instructions and any safety warnings given by them, especially any 'recall' type information about safety problems encountered with appliances some time after the particular model was first introduced onto the market.

176 If any safety defect is found as a result of the tests/examinations under regulation 26(9), the responsible person, and, if appropriate, the landlord for the premises should be notified as soon as possible. If neither is available, the gas supplier or transporter should be notified, as appropriate – see also regulation 34 concerning unsafe appliances.

Regulation 27

Flues

Regulation 27(1)

(1) No person shall install a gas appliance to any flue unless the flue is suitable and in a proper condition for the safe operation of the appliance.

ACOP

27(1)

177 Whenever an appliance is installed to a flue, the installer should ensure that the flue is adequate, suitable and effective for use with the appliance which it will serve. This requirement applies however the connection is made (eg it covers equally where an appliance is fitted to an existing flue, and where a flue is fitted to an existing appliance); in each case, the necessary tests and examinations should be carried out both before and after the appliance has been fitted. Requirements in Appendix 1 should be met, as applicable, and reference made to appropriate standards.

Guidance

27(1)

178 The requirements of Building Regulations concerning flues and chimneys should be met, where applicable. The fitting of a suitable terminal to any flue/chimney outlet is recommended, to assist products of combustion to escape, minimise downdraught and prevent entry of material, eg bird nests, which might cause blockage. In certain areas, eg where squirrels inhabit or birds such as jackdaws are known to roost, purpose-designed protection is essential to avoid such blockage (see paragraph 84).

179 It should not be assumed that previous satisfactory operation means that a flue will continue to be safe for use with another appliance, even of the same type. Appropriate tests and examinations should always be carried out, see Appendix 1. Guidance on types of appliance which require a flue to be fitted is given in the appropriate standards.

Regulation

27(2)–(3)

(2) No person shall install a flue pipe so that it enters a brick or masonry chimney in such a way that the seal between the flue pipe and chimney cannot be inspected.

(3) No person shall connect a gas appliance to a flue which is surrounded by an enclosure unless that enclosure is so sealed that any spillage of products of combustion cannot pass from the enclosure to any room or internal space other than the room or internal space in which the appliance is installed.

Guidance 27(2)–(3)

180 Where a false chimney breast or decorative canopy is fitted, it should be sealed from other rooms in the premises. Reference should be made to appropriate standards.

Regulation 27(4)

(4) No person shall install a power operated flue system for a gas appliance unless it safely prevents the operation of the appliance if the draught fails.

Guidance 27(4)

181 An interlock should be provided which will cut off the gas supply if the draught falls below a preset minimum standard for safe operation of the appliance, and prevent the gas supply being re-established unless safe to do so. The advice of the appliance/flue system manufacturer should be sought, as necessary, in respect of interlock design requirements and reference should be made to appropriate standards, eg concerning provision of manual reset facilities and interlocks with flame proving devices. See also regulation 32 and associated ACOP/guidance concerning flue dampers.

Regulation 27(5)

(5) No person shall install a flue other than in a safe position.

ACOP 27(5)

182 A flue (including any terminal) should be installed in a position which ensures that it will operate effectively and that products of combustion will safely disperse and not present a hazard to any person, whether in the premises in which the associated appliance is installed (eg by being located a safe distance from vents and openable windows), or in adjoining/neighbouring premises. The location needs to take into account any possible developments in neighbouring property, eg building extensions. Any flue should therefore be sited so as to discharge at a safe distance from any boundary with adjoining premises (see regulation 8 and Appendix 1); reference should be made to requirements in Building Regulations and appropriate standards, as applicable.

Regulation 28

Access

Regulation 28

No person shall install a gas appliance except in such a manner that it is readily accessible for operation, inspection and maintenance.

Guidance 28

183 Minimum clearance distances for operation, inspection and maintenance purposes are normally specified in manufacturer's instructions for installation of appliances.

Regulation 29

Manufacturer's instructions

Regulation 29

Any person who installs a gas appliance shall leave for the use of the owner or occupier of the premises in which the appliance is installed all instructions provided by the manufacturer accompanying the appliance.

Guidance 29

184 Requirements concerning manufacturer's instructions to accompany appliances are covered by the Gas Appliances (Safety) Regulations 1995 (see Appendix 3).

Regulation 30

Room-sealed appliances

Regulation 30(1)–(4)

(1) No person shall install a gas appliance in a room used or intended to be used as a bathroom or a shower room unless it is a room-sealed appliance.

Regulation

30(1)–(4)

(2) No person shall install a gas fire, other gas space heater or a gas water heater of more than 14 kilowatt gross heat input in a room used or intended to be used as sleeping accommodation unless the appliance is a room-sealed appliance.

(3) No person shall install a gas fire, other gas space heater or a gas water heater of 14 kilowatt gross heat input or less in a room used or intended to be used as sleeping accommodation and no person shall install an instantaneous water heater unless (in each case) -

(a) it is a room-sealed appliance; or
(b) it incorporates a safety control designed to shut down the appliance before there is a build up of a dangerous quantity of the products of combustion in the room concerned.

(4) The references in paragraphs (1) to (3) to a room used or intended to be used for the purpose therein referred to includes a reference to -

(a) a cupboard or compartment within such a room; or
(b) a cupboard, compartment or space adjacent to such a room if there is an air vent from the cupboard, compartment or space into such a room.

Guidance

30(1)–(4)

185 Under regulation 30(2), non-room-sealed appliances used for water heating, space heating and central heating of 14 kW or more gross heat input should not be installed in accommodation designed for sleeping purposes such as bedrooms, bed-sitting rooms and the sleeping areas of caravans. However, such heating appliances, of less than 14 kW gross heat input, may be fitted in these rooms/areas provided they incorporate a device which turns off the gas supply before a dangerous level of fumes can build up (regulation 30(3)). An instantaneous water heater, which is not room-sealed, may not be installed in any room unless it incorporates such a device.

186 The prohibitions in regulation 30 each extend to any cupboard or compartment which is accessed from the accommodation or room concerned (see regulation 30(4)). They also extend to any cupboard, compartment (eg cubicle) or space adjoining the accommodation or room concerned, where ventilation for safe operation of the appliance is provided via the accommodation or room concerned. Spaces adjoining the accommodation or room concerned where there is no air vent from the space into the room, ie which are provided with ventilation for safe operation of an appliance from another source, are not included in the prohibition. The rooms subject to the restrictions in regulation 30 are not only those actually being used as bathrooms, shower rooms or sleeping accommodation, but also those known to be intended for such use, at the time when the appliance is installed. The references to 'bathroom' and 'shower room' in this regulation include any room not purpose-built as such, but containing a functioning bath or shower, and the restrictions on appliance installation apply accordingly.

187 The prohibitions in regulation 30 also extend, in certain situations, to appliances fitted in rooms converted, or intended to be converted, by landlords into sleeping accommodation (see regulation 36(11)–(12)).

Regulation 31

Suspended appliances

Regulation

31

No person shall install a suspended gas appliance unless the installation pipework to which it is connected is so constructed and installed as to be capable of safely supporting the weight imposed on it and the appliance is designed to be so supported.

Guidance 31

188 The installation of appliances by suspension from installation pipework should be avoided, wherever practicable. Where this approach has to be considered, it should be ensured that the appliance is suitable for installation in this way and that the pipework is properly supported and capable of safely withstanding the weight imposed. Reference should be made to the appliance manufacturer instructions.

Regulation 32

Flue dampers

Regulation 32(1)–(3)

(1) Any person who installs an automatic damper to serve a gas appliance shall -

(a) ensure that the damper is so interlocked with the gas supply to the burner that burner operation is prevented in the event of failure of the damper when not in the open position; and
(b) immediately after installation examine the appliance and the damper to verify that they can be used together safely without constituting a danger to any person.

(2) No person shall install a manually operated damper to serve a domestic gas appliance.

(3) No person shall install a domestic gas appliance to a flue which incorporates a manually operated damper unless the damper is permanently fixed in the open position.

ACOP 32(1)–(3)

189 Reference should be made to appropriate standards and appliance manufacturer instructions (see Appendix 4).

Guidance 32(1)–(3)

190 An automatic damper may be used with a gas appliance subject to conditions in regulation 32(1) being satisfied. A damper system meeting these requirements will both prevent gas being supplied to the burner unless the damper is in the fully open position and provide for adequate pre-ignition purging and burner post-purging on flame failure; purging is particularly important for enclosed appliances where ignition of an unburned gas/air mixture in the combustion system has the potential to cause a serious explosion. See also paragraph 181 concerning power-operated flue systems.

191 The fitting of a manually operated damper system to serve a domestic gas appliance is prohibited under regulation 32(1) because, although it is possible to interlock the damper with the gas supply, an assured means of purging is not generally possible with such a system (see paragraph 190). Regulation 32(3) makes provision for an appliance to be fitted to an existing flue incorporating a manual damper, but only where the damper is permanently fixed in the open position. A manual damper may, for instance, often be present in a hearth used for burning coal or other solid fuel. Any such damper should be removed (this is often necessary for 'flame effect' fires), or permanently secured in the fully open position, so as to protect against the possibility of interference by a third party (such as the occupant) or of the damper falling into a closed position, eg as a result of corrosion damage.

Regulation 33

Testing of appliances

Regulation 33(1)

(1) Where a person installs a gas appliance at a time when gas is being supplied to the premises in which the appliance is installed, he shall immediately

Regulation 33(1)

thereafter test its connection to the installation pipework to verify that it is gastight and examine the appliance and the gas fittings and other works for the supply of gas and any flue or means of ventilation to be used in connection with the appliance for the purpose of ascertaining whether -

(a) the appliance has been installed in accordance with these Regulations;
(b) the operating pressure is as recommended by the manufacturer;
(c) the appliance has been installed with due regard to any manufacturer's instructions provided to accompany the appliance; and
(d) all gas safety controls are in proper working order.

ACOP 33(1)

192 Testing procedures should be in accordance with appropriate standards (see Appendices 1 and 4).

Regulation 33(2)

(2) Where a person carries out such testing and examination in relation to a gas appliance and adjustments are necessary to ensure compliance with the requirements specified in sub-paragraphs (a) to (d) of paragraph (1) above, he shall either carry out those adjustments or disconnect the appliance from the gas supply or seal off the appliance from the gas supply with an appropriate fitting.

ACOP 33(2)

193 Once the commissioning of an appliance is started, it should be either completed in full, leaving the appliance in a safe working condition, or the appliance should be disconnected or the gas supply to the appliance sealed off with an appropriate fitting, until tests and examinations can be fully completed at a later date. See also definition of 'appropriate fitting' in regulation 2(1).

Guidance 33(2)

194 In addition to disconnection/sealing off from the gas supply as in paragraph 193, a label needs to be attached to any appliance which has not been fully commissioned, indicating this to be the case and that appliance should not be reconnected to the gas supply, or the appropriate fitting sealing off the gas supply to the appliance removed, until the procedure has been safely completed. Where an appliance is disconnected, the outlet of every pipe to which it was connected should be sealed off in accordance with regulation 6(3).

Regulation 33(3)

(3) Where gas is not being supplied to any premises in which any gas appliance is installed -

(a) no person shall subsequently permit gas to pass into the appliance unless he has caused such testing, examination and adjustment as is specified in paragraphs (1) and (2) above to be carried out; and
(b) a person who subsequently provides a gas supply to those premises shall, unless he complies with sub-paragraph (a) above, ensure that the appliance is sealed off from the gas supply with an appropriate fitting.

ACOP 33(3)

195 A person who allows gas to flow into any appliance should ensure that gas fittings are purged and tested for safety, or the supply is sealed off with a fitting to the appropriate standard (see also definition of 'appropriate fitting' in regulation 2(1)).

Guidance 33(3)

196 This regulation applies when a premises is first being supplied with gas. In some cases, a gas supply may be provided some time before any installation work is done, or vice versa. Where this occurs, the supply or appliance should be properly capped so that no third party, eg the occupant, can easily interfere with it. The person finally connecting the supply to the appliance is responsible for testing and purging the system and appliance in accordance with regulations 22 and 33(1)–(2).

Guidance

33(3)

197 This regulation does not apply where gas has been temporarily cut off from an appliance, eg where the emergency control has been shut off or an over/under pressure valve has operated. Neither does it cover situations merely involving a change in supplier of gas to a premises.

Regulation 34

Regulation

34(1)–(2)

Use of appliances

(1) The responsible person for any premises shall not use a gas appliance or permit a gas appliance to be used if at any time he knows or has reason to suspect that it cannot be used without constituting a danger to any person.

(2) For the purposes of paragraph (1) above, the responsible person means the occupier of the premises, the owner of the premises and any person with authority for the time being to take appropriate action in relation to any gas fitting therein.

ACOP

34(1)–(2)

198 A responsible person must not use or allow the use of any appliance which it is known or suspected could constitute a danger to any person, and in particular danger of fire/explosion arising from gas leakage or carbon monoxide poisoning arising from inadequate flueing arrangements or fixed ventilation. An unsafe/dangerous appliance in this context means any appliance where both (a) and (b) which follow pertain:

(a) there is a design, construction, installation, modification, servicing/maintenance deficiency or other fault (eg maladjustment) in the gas appliance, associated flue/ventilation arrangement or a gas fitting/other works for the supply of gas to the appliance, which has, or is likely to result in:

(i) incomplete combustion of gas; or
(ii) removal of products of combustion not being safely carried out; or
(iii) insufficient oxygen being available for the occupants of the room/space in which the appliance is located; or
(iv) an accidental gas leakage; or
(v) other danger, eg of fire;

(b) the resulting leakage, inadequate combustion, inadequate removal of the products of combustion, insufficiency of oxygen or other danger has caused or is likely to cause death or serious injury.

Guidance

34(1)–(2)

199 Users and other persons with control over the use of gas appliances (as specified in regulation 34(2)) are required not to use or permit use of any gas appliance they know or suspect to be unsafe, eg when they have been told so by a competent gas engineer or emergency service provider. In the case of rented property this duty extends to tenants, landlords and managing agents. The requirement applies only to 'unsafe' appliances (see paragraph 198); it does not cover those which are merely 'sub-standard' and considered in need of minor improvements to bring them up to current standards.

200 General examples of the kinds of fault described in paragraph 198(a) which, if likely to cause death or serious injury, would be regarded as an 'unsafe' appliance, are given in Appendix 2. However, the level of risk, ie whether an appliance is 'dangerous' in a particular case, has to be a matter for judgement by a competent person, based on their knowledge and experience, and taking into account the specific circumstances. Further information is given in industry guidance on 'unsafe situations' procedures, eg as issued by Gas Safe Register. See also regulation 37 and associated guidance, concerning action in event of a gas escape.

Guidance

201 If a gas engineer discovers an unsafe gas appliance, the user and, if different, the owner of the appliance (in rented accommodation, the landlord; or managing agent, where the landlord is absent or has entrusted the agent to deal with gas safety matters on his behalf) should be informed, in writing, that the appliance is unsafe and that continued use is an offence. The engineer should seek to persuade the user/owner to allow them to repair or disconnect the appliance but the engineer has no legal power to take such action if the user/owner disagrees. If consent for such action is not obtained, the appliance should be suitably labelled as being unsafe and that continued use is an offence; with the agreement of the responsible person, the appliance shut-off device (if one is fitted) should be closed. Irrespective of any action taken by the gas engineer, the obligation rests on the responsible person(s) not to use, or allow the use of any unsafe gas appliance.

202 Where agreement of the responsible person cannot be obtained for repair or disconnection of an unsafe appliance, the engineer is advised, in the case of an appliance supplied with LPG, to contact the gas supplier or, in any other case including natural gas, the Gas Emergency Freephone Number 0800 111 999. In an emergency situation a public gas transporter has powers to enter property and take action to avert danger to life (and property) under the Gas Safety (Rights of Entry) Regulations 1996. In the case of LPG, a contractual right of entry may exist between the supplier and customer.

203 In addition to requiring reports of specified gas incidents, the Reporting of Injuries, Diseases and Dangerous Occurrences Regulations 1995 (RIDDOR) require a report of certain dangerous appliances to be made to HSE (see RIDDOR regulation 6(2)). A report will generally be required where disconnection of an appliance is considered to be necessary, as described in paragraph 201.

34(1)–(2)

Regulation

(3) Any person engaged in carrying out any work in relation to a gas main, service pipe, service pipework, gas storage vessel or gas fitting who knows or has reason to suspect that any gas appliance cannot be used without constituting a danger to any person shall forthwith take all reasonably practicable steps to inform the responsible person for the premises in which the appliance is situated and, where different, the owner of the appliance or, where neither is reasonably practicable, in the case of an appliance supplied with liquefied petroleum gas, the supplier of gas to the appliance, or, in any other case, the transporter.

(4) In paragraph (3) above, the expression "work" shall be construed as if, in the definition of "work" in regulation 2(1) above, every reference to a gas fitting were a reference to a gas main, service pipe, service pipework, gas storage vessel or gas fitting.

34(3)–(4)

Guidance

204 Regulation 34(3) places a duty on a person engaged in any work specified in regulation 34(4), eg a gas engineer, who becomes aware of an unsafe/dangerous appliance, to take steps to inform the responsible person for the premises concerned, such as the landlord/managing agent of rented accommodation, and (where different) the gas appliance owner, ie as described in paragraph 201. Where none of these persons is available or readily contactable, the gas supplier or transporter (as appropriate) is required to be notified to enable any necessary action to be taken to make the appliance safe. Details of the gas supplier/transporter emergency gas service may be found on a notice near the meter, or where there is no meter, the emergency control (see regulations 9 and 15). If there is no notice, or the relevant information is not given, the information may be found in the telephone directory.

34(3)–(4)

PART F MAINTENANCE

Regulation 35

Duties of employers and self-employed persons

Regulation 35

It shall be the duty of every employer or self-employed person to ensure that any gas appliance, installation pipework or flue installed at any place of work under his control is maintained in a safe condition so as to prevent risk of injury to any person.

Guidance

205 The duty to maintain appliances, flues and installation pipework is linked to other related workplace safety responsibilities, eg under the Health and Safety at Work etc Act 1974 or the Provision and Use of Work Equipment Regulations 1998 (see Appendix 3); this provision only applies to workplaces falling within the scope of the Regulations (see regulations 2(4)–(5)), but similar duties are imposed by separate safety legislation in other places, eg factories (see paragraph 42). The duty under regulation 35 extends to certain mobile and portable appliances, eg LPG space heaters (see definition of gas appliance in regulation 2(1)). Maintenance of service pipework is not covered by regulation 35, but duties in this respect are applied under the general provisions of the Health and Safety at Work etc Act 1974 and related legislation (see Appendix 3).

206 Effective routine maintenance normally involves an ongoing programme of regular/periodic examinations, and remedial action, as necessary. For specific requirements reference should be made, as appropriate, to manufacturer instructions for servicing of appliances. Where detailed information is not available, the engineer may need to check the physical condition of the appliance, air vent(s), flue and installation pipework for deterioration, carry out performance tests, and take the necessary remedial action. For appliances and flues, maintenance should address the points in Appendix 1; additional aspects may need to be addressed in a particular case, eg dismantling and cleaning burners and inspection and/or cleaning of any combustion fan, as appropriate (see also regulation 26(9) for tests/examinations required after any work is done on an appliance). In the case of some gas equipment and fittings (eg flexible pipework, certain protective devices etc), where inadequate maintenance could cause failure in a dangerous way, a formal system of planned preventative maintenance might be necessary. This aims to prevent failures occurring while equipment is in use and involves a system of written instructions, eg based on appliance/fitting manufacturer's instructions, used to initiate inspection, testing and periodic replacement or refurbishing of components or equipment before they reach the end of their useful life. Further information is given in the HSE publication *Work equipment. Provision and Use of Work Equipment Regulations 1998. Approved Code of Practice and Guidance*, see Appendix 4.

207 Where non-domestic premises such as public houses or offices are leased as workplaces, employer's duties under regulation 35 may interface with landlord's responsibilities under section 4 of the Health and Safety at Work etc Act 1974, eg for maintenance of gas heating appliances. In these situations, close co-operation and clear allocation of responsibilities is essential to ensure that requirements are fully met and no gaps in safety cover can arise. The landlord and tenant (ie employer/self-employed person) may come to a contractual arrangement in such cases, and such action is recommended to ensure responsibilities are clearly and unambiguously defined (see also paragraph 214 concerning duties in relation to mixed domestic/non-domestic premises).

Regulation 36 — Duties of landlords

(1) In this regulation -

"landlord" means -

(a) in England and Wales -

    (i) where the relevant premises are occupied under a lease, the person for the time being entitled to the reversion expectant on that lease or who, apart from any statutory tenancy, would be entitled to possession of the premises; and

    (ii) where the relevant premises are occupied under a licence, the licensor, save that where the licensor is himself a tenant in respect of those premises, it means the person referred to in paragraph (i) above;

(b) in Scotland, the person for the time being entitled to the landlord's interest under a lease;

"lease" means -

(a) a lease for a term of less than 7 years; and
(b) a tenancy for a periodic term; and
(c) any statutory tenancy arising out of a lease or tenancy referred to in sub-paragraphs (a) or (b) above,

and in determining whether a lease is one which falls within sub-paragraph (a) above -

    (i) in England and Wales, any part of the term which falls before the grant shall be left out of account and the lease shall be treated as a lease for a term commencing with the grant;

    (ii) a lease which is determinable at the option of the lessor before the expiration of 7 years from the commencement of the term shall be treated as a lease for a term of less than 7 years;

    (iii) a lease (other than a lease to which sub-paragraph (b) above applies) shall not be treated as a lease for a term of less than 7 years if it confers on the lessee an option for renewal for a term which, together with the original term, amounts to 7 years or more; and

    (iv) a "lease" does not include a mortgage term;

"relevant gas fitting" means -

(a) any gas appliance (other than an appliance which the tenant is entitled to remove from the relevant premises) or any installation pipework installed in any relevant premises; and

(b) any gas appliance or installation pipework which, directly or indirectly, serves the relevant premises and which either -

    (i) is installed in any part of premises in which the landlord has an estate or interest; or

    (ii) is owned by the landlord or is under his control,

except that it shall not include any gas appliance or installation pipework exclusively used in a part of premises occupied for non-residential purposes.

> | Regulation |
> | --- |
> | 36(1)–(10) |

"*relevant premises*" *means premises or any part of premises occupied, whether exclusively or not, for residential purposes (such occupation being in consideration of money or money's worth) under -*

(a) *a lease; or*
(b) *a licence;*

"*statutory tenancy*" *means -*

(a) *in England and Wales, a statutory tenancy within the meaning of the Rent Act 1977*[a] *and the Rent (Agriculture) Act 1976*[b]; *and*
(b) *in Scotland, a statutory tenancy within the meaning of the Rent (Scotland) Act 1984*[c], *a statutory assured tenancy within the meaning of the Housing (Scotland) Act 1988*[d] *or a secure tenancy within the meaning of the Housing (Scotland) Act 1987*[e];

"*tenant*" *means a person who occupies relevant premises being -*

(a) *in England and Wales -*

   (i) *where the relevant premises are so occupied under a lease, the person for the time being entitled to the term of that lease; and*
   (ii) *where the relevant premises are so occupied under a licence, the licensee;*

(b) *in Scotland, the person for the time being entitled to the tenant's interest under a lease.*

(2) *Every landlord shall ensure that there is maintained in safe condition -*

(a) *any relevant gas fitting; and*
(b) *any flue which serves any relevant gas fitting,*

so as to prevent the risk of injury to any person in lawful occupation of relevant premises.

(3) *Without prejudice to the generality of paragraph 2 above, a landlord shall -*

(a) *ensure that each appliance and flue to which that duty extends is checked for safety within 12 months of being installed and at intervals of not more than 12 months since it was last checked for safety (whether such check was made pursuant to these Regulations or not);*
(b) *in the case of a lease commencing after the coming into force of these Regulations, ensure that each appliance and flue to which the duty extends has been checked for safety within a period of 12 months before the lease commences or has been or is so checked within 12 months after the appliance or flue has been installed, whichever is later; and*
(c) *ensure that a record in respect of any appliance or flue so checked is made and retained for a period of 2 years from the date of that check, which record shall include the following information -*

(a) 1977 c.42.
(b) 1976 c.80.
(c) 1984 c.58.
(d) 1988 c.43.
(e) 1987 c.26.

> **Regulation**
>
> (i) the date on which the appliance or flue was checked;
> (ii) the address of the premises at which the appliance or flue is installed;
> (iii) the name and address of the landlord of the premises (or, where appropriate, his agent) at which the appliance or flue is installed;
> (iv) a description of and the location of each appliance or flue checked;
> (v) any defect identified;
> (vi) any remedial action taken;
> (vii) confirmation that the check undertaken complies with the requirements of paragraph (9) below;
> (viii) the name and signature of the individual carrying out the check; and
> (ix) the registration number with which that individual, or his employer, is registered with a body approved by the Executive for the purposes of regulation 3(3) of these Regulations.
>
> (4) Every landlord shall ensure that any work in relation to a relevant gas fitting or any check of a gas appliance or flue carried out pursuant to paragraphs (2) or (3) above is carried out by, or by an employee of, a member of a class of persons approved for the time being by the Health and Safety Executive for the purposes of regulation 3(3) of these Regulations.
>
> (5) The record referred to in paragraph 3(c) above, or a copy thereof, shall be made available upon request and upon reasonable notice for the inspection of any person in lawful occupation of relevant premises who may be affected by the use or operation of any appliance to which the record relates.
>
> (6) Notwithstanding paragraph (5) above, every landlord shall ensure that -
>
> (a) a copy of the record made pursuant to the requirements of paragraph 3(c) above is given to each existing tenant of premises to which the record relates within 28 days of the date of the check; and
> (b) a copy of the last record made in respect of each appliance or flue is given to any new tenant of premises to which the record relates before that tenant occupies those premises save that, in respect of a tenant whose right to occupy those premises is for a period not exceeding 28 days, a copy of the record may instead be prominently displayed within those premises.
>
> (7) Where there is no relevant gas appliance in any room occupied or to be occupied by the tenant in relevant premises, the landlord may, instead of ensuring that a copy of the record referred to in paragraph (6) above is given to the tenant, ensure that there is displayed in a prominent position in the premises (from such time as a copy would have been required to have been given to the tenant under that paragraph), a copy of the record with a statement endorsed on it that the tenant is entitled to have his own copy of the record on request to the landlord at an address specified in the statement; and on any such request being made, the landlord shall give to the tenant a copy of the record as soon as is reasonably practicable.
>
> (8) A copy of the record given to a tenant pursuant to paragraph (6)(b) above need not contain a copy of the signature of the individual carrying out the check if the copy of the record contains a statement that another copy containing a copy of such signature is available for inspection by the tenant on request to the landlord at the address specified in the statement, and on any such request being made the landlord shall make such a copy available for inspection as soon as is practicable.
>
> **36(1)–(10)**

> **Regulation**
>
> **36(1)–(10)**
>
> *(9) A safety check carried out pursuant to paragraph (3) above shall include, but shall not be limited to, an examination of the matters referred to in sub-paragraphs (a) to (d) of regulation 26(9) of these Regulations.*
>
> *(10) Nothing done or agreed to be done by a tenant of relevant premises or by any other person in lawful occupation of them in relation to the maintenance or checking of a relevant gas fitting or flue in the premises (other than one in part of premises occupied for non-residential purposes) shall be taken into account in determining whether a landlord has discharged his obligations under this regulation (except in so far as it relates to access to that gas fitting or flue for the purposes of such maintenance or checking).*

Guidance

36(1)–(10)

Application

208 Regulation 36 places important duties on most landlords of domestic property to ensure that gas appliances and flues are maintained in a safe condition, annual safety checks are carried out, and records are kept and issued (or in certain cases displayed) to tenants. These duties are in addition to the more general ones that landlords have under the Health and Safety at Work etc Act 1974 and the Management of Health and Safety at Work Regulations 1999.

209 The meaning of 'landlord' in regulation 36(1) effectively applies the requirements to a wide range of accommodation (occupied under a licence, or a lease as defined in the Regulations), including residential premises provided for rent by local authorities, housing associations, private sector landlords, housing co-operatives and hostels. Rooms let in bed-sit accommodation, private households, and bed and breakfast accommodation are also covered, as is rented holiday accommodation such as chalets, cottages, flats, caravans and narrowboats on inland waterways. The duties apply to landlords providing residential accommodation for occupation by others on the basis of a lease for less than seven years, a tenancy agreement for a periodic term, or a licence. The lease period of less than seven years reflects provisions of the Landlord and Tenant Act 1985 and Scottish housing legislation which impose an implied covenant on a landlord to repair installations for space heating and water heating in a 'dwelling house'. Regulation 36 does not apply simply because a lease longer than seven years has partly expired, leaving a residue of less than seven years duration. Properties are not brought within scope merely because they are occupied under the terms of a mortgage, but premises subject to shared ownership may be caught if other conditions are satisfied.

210 Landlords using agents to manage properties need to ensure that the management contract clearly specifies who is responsible for carrying out the maintenance and safety check duties, and keeping associated records. Where a breach of these Regulations by a landlord is shown to arise from the act or default of a managing agent, the agent may be liable to legal action under this regulation by virtue of section 36(1) of the Health and Safety at Work etc Act 1974, regardless of whether or not separate proceedings are taken against the landlord.

211 In the case of sub-let accommodation, the 'original' landlord may retain duties which overlap with those acquired by the person who sub-lets. In these cases, dutyholders need to take effective steps (eg by close co-operation, and clear allocation of responsibilities under contractual arrangements) to ensure requirements are fully met. However, licensors (ie 'sub-letters') of premises who are themselves tenants of those premises are not regarded as landlords in this context and do not have obligations under regulation 36. This means that a tenant allowing others to share accommodation in return for 'rent' does not acquire duties under the regulation; these remain with their landlord.

Guidance

212 Regulation 36(10) requires landlords generally to act independently of tenants in meeting their obligations under regulation 36 (except with regard to gaining access for carrying out maintenance/safety checks). Duties, apart from those relating to a relevant gas fitting or associated flue in part of premises occupied for non-residential purposes (see paragraph 214), may not be delegated in any way to a tenant, eg by the landlord asking a tenant to make the necessary arrangements for work to be carried out. Further, a tenancy agreement, such as a full repairing and insuring lease, cannot be used to transfer these responsibilities to a tenant. However, tenants need to co-operate as necessary, eg by promptly reporting any appliance, flue or installation pipework defect to the landlord or managing agent.

213 All reasonable steps should be taken by landlords (including through tenancy agreements) to ensure access to property for safety checks and maintenance work to be done, this may involve giving written notice to a tenant (eg by recorded delivery) explaining the reasons why access is required and requesting arrangements to be made (at a mutually agreed date/time); follow-up action, including personal visits, might be required, for instance, if there is no response to written request. Tenants should co-operate with landlords in allowing the necessary access to their accommodation. However, landlords should keep a record of their action in case a tenant refuses entry and it is necessary to demonstrate the steps taken to discharge their duties (see regulation 39). Action to gain access does not involve making arrangements for forced entry into property. See also paragraph 245.

214 Regulation 36(10) allows flexibility for landlords to make arrangements, eg by contract, with tenants for discharging maintenance/safety check duties in respect of a relevant gas fitting or flue installed in part of premises occupied for non-residential premises (see paragraphs 223–225). This means, for instance, where a gas appliance, such as a central heating boiler, is installed in the 'bar area' of a public house, the landlord of the building (eg brewery company) may make contractual arrangements for the bar manager to ensure requirements under regulation 36 are met, even where the manager is a tenant of a residential part of the premises, such as a flat, also served by the appliance. In the case of such mixed residential/non-residential property, where there may be an interface between landlord's duties, eg for maintenance of gas appliances (under regulation 36 and section 4 of the Health and Safety at Work etc Act 1974) and those of employers/self-employed persons (under regulation 35), close co-operation and clear definition of duties in this way is essential to ensure requirements are fully met and there are no gaps in safety cover (see also paragraph 207).

215 Duties under regulation 36 do not apply to any gas appliance or installation pipework used <u>exclusively</u> in a part of premises occupied for non-residential purposes. However, landlord's duties for maintenance under section 4 of the Health and Safety at Work etc Act 1974 (HSW Act) may in some cases extend to such equipment, and where the part of the premises concerned is a workplace, maintenance requirements under regulation 35, together with relevant duties under the HSW Act and related Regulations (eg Provision and Use of Work Equipment Regulations 1998) are applicable. Any gas appliance or installation pipework installed in a part of premises used for non-domestic purposes, but (also) serving residential accommodation (eg a central heating boiler) is regarded as a 'relevant gas fitting' and therefore covered by regulation 36 (see paragraphs 223–224), but allowance is made for display of safety check records in some cases (paragraph 222 refers).

Maintenance and safety check duties

216 Regulation 36 imposes two <u>main duties</u> on landlords, concerning (a) annual safety checks on gas appliances/flues, and (b) ongoing maintenance; it is important

36(1)–(10)

Guidance

to recognise that, although related, these duties are separate and distinct (eg see paragraph 219). Unlike most of the other regulations, both duties extend to certain mobile and portable appliances, eg LPG cabinet heaters (see definition of gas appliance in regulation 2(1)); further information on appliances, flues and pipework covered is given in paragraphs 223–225. Although regulation 36 does not apply to any gas appliance a tenant is entitled to remove from relevant premises (eg an appliance owned by a tenant), in discharging duties, landlords need to take account of any appliance left by a tenant (ie when a lease comes to an end) which the landlord decides to retain in the premises.

217 Regulation 36(2) requires gas appliances, flues and installation pipework to be maintained in a safe condition. Effective maintenance of gas appliances normally involves an ongoing programme of regular/periodic inspections, together with any necessary remedial work. Specific maintenance requirements are sometimes defined in manufacturer instructions for servicing appliances. In the absence of such information, a gas engineer may need to check the physical condition of the appliance, installation pipework, air vent(s) and any flue for deterioration, carry out performance tests, and take the necessary remedial action. Appendix 1 gives information on general points to be addressed for appliances and flues but additional aspects may require attention in a particular case, eg dismantling/cleaning of burners and inspection/cleaning of any combustion fan, as appropriate.

218 The appliance/flue safety check under regulation 36(3)(a) must be carried out on an 'annual' basis. Regulation 36(3)(b) provides for situations where a 'lease' commences (after these Regulations came into force), subsequent to a period when any gas appliance/flue in the premises concerned was not subject to regulation 36(3)(a), eg because the property was left unoccupied. In such cases, a safety check needs to be (or have been) carried out within 12 months prior to the commencement date of the lease or within 12 months of the date when the appliance or flue was installed, whichever is later. Subsequent safety checks must then be carried out at intervals of not more than one year, starting from the date of that check, for the duration of the lease. Although the landlord's safety check under regulation 36(3)(a) may be carried out at any time within one year of the appliance installation date (and within one-year intervals thereafter), it is important to recognise that this check is additional to examinations under regulation 26 (eg when an appliance is first installed or subsequent work is done), and checks required for ongoing maintenance purposes under regulation 36(2), for instance, before a new tenancy is commenced (see paragraph 226).

219 The safety check needs to address, as a minimum, the points given in regulation 26(9) – see Appendix 1. It may need to include extra examinations/tests in a particular case; this will normally be for the engineer to assess. Although it is recommended that an annual service inspection includes the points required by a safety check, landlords should not assume that this is the case; neither should it be assumed that carrying out annual safety checks will be sufficient to provide effective maintenance. The advice of a competent gas engineer should be sought where necessary on action required. Installation pipework is not covered by the annual safety check but it is recommended that a test for soundness on the whole gas system, including installation pipework, together with visual examination (as far as is reasonably practicable) of the pipework, be made at the same time as the safety check. Landlords should also ensure that installation pipework is properly examined/tested whenever any damage or associated problem, eg suspected gas leak, is reported by a tenant.

220 The safety check should be carried out by someone who is, or is employed by a member of a class of persons approved by HSE under regulation 3(3), eg a Gas Safe-registered engineer, whether or not it includes 'work' as defined in regulation

36(1)–(10)

Guidance

2(1) (this will normally be the case). The safety check record should contain the information specified in regulation 36(3)(c). The appliance/flue covered by a safety check should be clearly and unambiguously identified, eg by make or model, as necessary. A safety check record should never be issued unless and until all the required tests/examinations have been completed. The engineer should investigate any evidence of unsafe operation and report to the responsible person(s), see regulation 34; the Reporting of Injuries, Diseases and Dangerous Occurrences Regulations 1995 (RIDDOR) require a report of certain dangerous appliances to be made to HSE (see RIDDOR regulation 6(2)). A landlord should take prompt action to correct any defect shown on a safety check record, which is not remedied at the time of the safety check; and where there is any suspicion that an appliance may be dangerous, the landlord or other responsible person for the premises should ensure that the appliance concerned is not used until the defect(s) have been remedied (see regulation 34).

221 Landlords should maintain a record of each safety check, a copy of which should be issued to any existing tenant within 28 days of the check and, in the case of any new tenancy, to the prospective tenant prior to occupation of the premises. In addition, regulation 36(4) requires the safety check record or a copy to be made available on request (at reasonable notice) for inspection by tenants concerned. In case of a new tenancy, regulation 36(8) provides for a copy of a record not containing the signature of the engineer, eg a computerised record, to be issued by the landlord. However, the tenant has the right to inspect a signed copy, on request.

222 For occupancies under 28 days, such as rented holiday accommodation, a copy of the safety check record may be posted in a prominent position in the premises, eg mobile home or caravan, concerned. In relevant premises, eg college halls of residence, boarding schools, houses in multiple occupation etc, where a gas appliance is not located in any room occupied or to be occupied by a tenant (whether for exclusive or 'common' use such as a communal living room, hallway, kitchen or bathroom), a similar option is available under regulation 36(7) to display the safety check record in a prominent position. This would, for example, apply to a gas boiler serving a central heating system, which is located in a boiler house or compartment separate to any room occupied by a tenant. In such cases, the notice should be posted centrally; it should indicate that an individual copy of the safety check is available to any tenant on request, and specify where this may be obtained. Landlords need to inform tenants of the location of this notice and of the option of obtaining an individual copy of a safety check record, at the start of any new tenancy. They should ensure that any record displayed under regulation 36(6) or (7) is maintained in a legible condition.

223 In addition to gas appliances installed in 'relevant premises' (see regulation 36(1)), the safety check duty applies to any appliance, eg a central heating boiler, directly or indirectly serving relevant premises. This includes appliances which, in addition, may serve premises, or parts of premises, otherwise excluded from regulation 36 – see definition of 'relevant gas fitting'. Such appliances may include those installed in areas of property where there is 'common' occupancy (ie by tenants covered by these Regulations and possibly other persons as well), such as 'communal' living rooms, kitchens and bathrooms in houses in multiple occupation. However, any gas appliance <u>exclusively</u> used in a part of premises occupied for non-residential purposes is not covered. See also paragraph 214 concerning provisions for allowing landlords to make arrangements with tenants for discharging maintenance/safety check duties in respect of a relevant gas fitting or flue installed in part of premises occupied for non-residential purposes.

224 The maintenance duty covers the same range of appliances as the safety check requirement but also extends to installation pipework, and includes appliances/pipework serving relevant premises, but not any <u>exclusively</u> used in

36(1)–(10)

| Guidance

36(1)–(10) | 'non-residential' areas. As with appliances, this means that pipework forming part of a system which also serves premises outside the scope of the regulation may be covered, as may that serving certain gas appliances, not themselves subject to regulation 36, eg appliances owned by tenants but installed in relevant premises.

225 Both the maintenance and safety check duties cover flues, including those serving gas appliances installed in relevant premises, as well as flues fitted to appliances directly or indirectly serving the relevant premises. All sections of a flue, ie both those specific and local to appliances as well as 'common' parts of flues (eg associated with Se- and U- ducts, and Shunt flues) need to be covered under maintenance and safety check duties. Landlords should make appropriate arrangements with tenants and occupiers of any other property through which a flue passes, to enable access for inspection, tests and maintenance work to be carried out (see paragraph 213 and Appendix 1).

226 When tenants vacate premises, landlords need to ensure that gas fittings/ appliances are safe before re-letting. Tenants may have removed appliances unsafely (eg leaving open-ended pipes, having shut off the emergency control valve), or left their appliances in place. Appropriate checks should be carried out and any unsafe equipment rectified or removed before a new tenancy begins – see also paragraphs 216 and 218. It is also recommended that installation pipework be inspected and tested for soundness before property is re-let. |

Regulation

36(11)–(12)

(11) Every landlord shall ensure that in any room occupied or to be occupied as sleeping accommodation by a tenant in relevant premises there is not fitted a relevant gas fitting of a type the installation of which would contravene regulation 30(2) or (3) of these Regulations.

(12) Paragraph (11) above shall not apply in relation to a room which since before the coming into force of these Regulations has been occupied or intended to be occupied as sleeping accommodation.

Guidance

36(11)–(12)

227 Under regulation 36(11)–(12), a landlord must ensure that where a room is, or is intended to be used as sleeping accommodation, there is no gas appliance fitted, the installation of which would be prohibited under regulation 30(2) or (3). This means, for instance, that any existing appliance of the type specified there, eg certain gas heaters and instantaneous water heaters, should be removed from any room which is to be converted into sleeping accommodation. However, these requirements do not apply retrospectively, and relate only to those conversions to rooms on or after the date the Regulations came into force (see regulation 1).

PART G MISCELLANEOUS

Regulation 37 Escape of gas

Guidance 37

228 This regulation is primarily restricted to <u>LPG and certain other fuel gases</u> (see definition of 'gas' in regulation 2(1)) which do not consist wholly or mainly of methane; it does not cover an escape of natural gas from any network – paragraph 241 refers. The requirements also extend to an actual or suspected escape or emission of fumes, ie products of combustion containing carbon monoxide (CO), from an appliance using a gas other than natural gas (see regulation 37(8)). Where a gas escape or emission of fumes arises from a dangerous appliance, requirements under regulation 34 also need to be met. Action in the case of a natural gas escape, or suspected emission of carbon monoxide from a natural gas appliance (where, in either case, natural gas is supplied from a network) is covered under regulation 7 of the Gas Safety (Management) Regulations 1996. Any gas escape or incident involving emission of carbon monoxide from a dangerous appliance should be reported, as applicable, under the Reporting of Injuries, Diseases and Dangerous Occurrences Regulations 1995 (see Appendix 3).

229 Regulation 37 extends to certain premises, eg factories, mines and quarries, otherwise excluded from GSIUR (see regulation 2(4)). For the meaning of 'supplier', reference should be made to regulation 2(1)–(2); see also regulation 37(6) concerning sub-contracting to other emergency service providers.

Regulation 37(1)

(1) *Where any gas escapes from any pipe of a gas supplier or from any pipe, other gas fitting or gas storage vessel used by a person supplied with gas by a gas supplier, the supplier of the gas shall, within 12 hours of being so informed of the escape, prevent the gas escaping (whether by cutting off the supply of gas to any premises or otherwise).*

Guidance 37(1)

230 Gas suppliers/emergency service providers, for gas supplies other than natural gas in a network, need to make arrangements to ensure that reports of emergencies can be received and responded to 24 hours a day. In order to avoid delays, responders to emergency calls need an outline script enabling them to:

(a) establish the precise location of the emergency;
(b) in case of a fuel gas escape:

    (i) establish if and how the leak may be controlled, ie by isolating an emergency control or cylinder valve(s), as appropriate;
    (ii) advise callers how to turn off the gas at the emergency control/cylinder valve(s) and confirm that this has been done; except where this may be dangerous, eg requiring entry into a confined space where there is a smell of gas, when the advice should be not to take such action but instead to vacate premises;
    (iii) advise callers to open doors and windows to ventilate the property and not to smoke, or use electrical appliances/other sources of ignition;

(c) establish whether there are fumes (escape of carbon monoxide into the room), and if it is possible to identify the appliance emitting the fumes;
(d) advise callers where an escape of CO is suspected, of the immediate steps to be taken, ie to turn off appliances which may be emitting CO (all the appliances in the room/area, where the defective appliance cannot be identified), ventilate property to disperse CO and not to use the appliances concerned again until they have been checked by a competent gas engineer who meets the requirements of regulation 3, eg who is Gas Safe-registered.

Guidance

37(1)

231 In case of a fuel gas escape, the gas supplier/emergency service provider should attend the emergency, as soon as is reasonably practicable after receiving a report of the escape. Once at the emergency, appropriate steps should be taken to bring the situation under control, and make it safe as quickly as possible. The 12-hour period specified in regulation 37(1) is the maximum time that should normally be taken to stop gas escaping.

232 Gas suppliers/emergency service providers need to ensure that they:

(a) are registered, as appropriate, with a body approved by HSE under regulation 3, eg Gas Safe Register, for work on gas fittings and installation pipework;
(b) employ an adequate number of competent operatives with sufficient knowledge, appropriate equipment, practical skill and experience to deal with all foreseeable emergency situations (see paragraph 47);
(c) establish written procedures for operatives to follow.

233 The primary duty on gas suppliers/emergency service providers in the event of an emergency is to take action to ensure the situation is made safe. They need to:

(a) respond to reports of fuel gas escapes and take action as necessary to make the situation safe by preventing gas from escaping; and/or
(b) respond to reports of suspected or actual CO escapes and advise on the action to be taken to make the situation safe.

234 Calls relating to escapes of gas other than natural gas, eg LPG, may be misdirected to National Grid plc. Gas suppliers may wish to consider arrangements for liaison with National Grid plc, in respect of such calls.

Regulation

37(2)–(4)

(2) If the responsible person for any premises knows or has reason to suspect that gas is escaping into those premises, he shall immediately take all reasonable steps to cause the supply of gas to be shut off at such place as may be necessary to prevent further escape of gas.

(3) If gas continues to escape into those premises after the supply of gas has been shut off or when a smell of gas persists, the responsible person for the premises discovering such escape or smell shall immediately give notice of the escape or smell to the supplier of the gas.

(4) Where an escape of gas has been stopped by shutting off the supply, no person shall cause or permit the supply to be re-opened (other than in the course of repair) until all necessary steps have been taken to prevent a recurrence of such escape.

Guidance

37(2)–(4)

235 Where a fuel gas escape is suspected or known to be occurring, the responsible person (see definition in regulation 2(1)) should take immediate action to cause the emergency control or gas cylinder shut-off valve(s), as appropriate, to be closed; except where this would be dangerous, eg requiring entry into a confined space where there is a smell of gas, when the premises should instead be evacuated. If gas continues to escape, the responsible person should immediately notify the supplier emergency gas service that there is a suspected escape of gas. In any case of a gas escape, doors and windows should be opened to ventilate the property and all sources of ignition, eg smoking or use of electrical equipment, should be avoided. The gas supply should not be reinstated until remedial action has been taken and appropriate checks made (eg that appliance isolation valves are closed, as appropriate) to avoid a further escape of gas.

236 In the case of a suspected escape of carbon monoxide (CO) the responsible person should turn off any appliances suspected of emitting CO, open doors and

Guidance

37(2)–(4)

windows to ventilate the property and contact the gas supplier emergency service immediately. However, where a particular appliance is known to be the source of the escape, the responsible person should ensure that it is not used and contact someone who is, or is employed by a member of an HSE approved class of persons under regulation 3(3), eg a Gas Safe-registered engineer, to repair, replace, or otherwise make safe the appliance (see also regulation 34).

237 The name and means of contacting the supplier emergency gas service may be found on a notice near the meter, or where there is no meter, the emergency gas control (see regulations 9 and 15, and associated guidance). If there is no notice, or the relevant information is not given, details of the gas supplier may be found in the telephone directory.

238 Similar action to the above is required under the Gas Safety (Management) Regulations 1996, for any natural gas escape, or suspected emission of carbon monoxide from a natural gas appliance (where the natural gas is supplied from a network). In such cases, the Gas Emergency Freephone Number 0800 111 999 should be contacted.

Regulation

37(5)

(5) In any proceedings for an offence under paragraph (1) above it shall be a defence for the supplier of the gas to prove that it was not reasonably practicable for him effectually to prevent the gas from escaping within the period of 12 hours referred to in that paragraph, and that he did effectually prevent the escape of gas as soon as it was reasonably practicable for him to do so.

Guidance

37(5)

239 There may be circumstances, eg a major leak from a storage tank, when it may not be feasible to stop the gas escape within 12 hours. Gas suppliers will, however, need to ensure that the situation is brought under control and made safe as soon as is reasonably practicable and in any event within 12 hours, in order to meet the requirements of this regulation. Where it is not possible to stop leakage within 12 hours, gas suppliers/emergency service providers will need to demonstrate that they took all reasonable steps to do so.

Regulation

37(6)

(6) Nothing in paragraphs (1) and (5) above shall prevent the supplier of the gas appointing another person to act on his behalf to prevent an escape of gas supplied by that supplier.

Guidance

37(6)

240 Gas suppliers may sub-contract emergency service provision to another person or organisation (the 'emergency service provider'), eg in the interests of providing a more local and immediate response in a particular area or at a specific site. This may, for instance, be especially relevant for local companies supplying gas in cylinders which may be used over a wide geographical area. However, where an emergency service provider is appointed in this way, the primary responsibility remains with the supplier concerned (see paragraphs 18–20 for allocation of duties in particular circumstances).

Regulation

37(7)

(7) Nothing in paragraphs (1) to (6) above shall apply to an escape of gas from a network (within the meaning of regulation 2 of the Gas Safety (Management) Regulations 1996[a]) or from a gas fitting supplied with gas from a network.

(a) *S.I. 1996/551*

Guidance

37(7)

241 This regulation limits requirements in regulation 37(1)–(6) primarily to LPG and certain other gases (see definition of 'gas' in regulation 2(1)) which are <u>not</u> wholly or mainly composed of methane. The exclusion of an escape of natural gas from any 'network' effectively means that virtually all escapes of natural gas

Guidance 37(7)

will not be covered under this regulation; the only exception is where such an escape occurs from a 'stand alone' network of pipes which conveys gas only to non-domestic premises falling within these Regulations, eg an office block. In all other cases, escapes of natural gas are covered by requirements under regulation 7 of the Gas Safety (Management) Regulations 1996; action in case of an emission or suspected emission of carbon monoxide from a natural gas appliance is similarly covered.

Regulation 37(8)

(8) In this regulation any reference to an escape of gas from a gas fitting includes a reference to an escape or emission of carbon monoxide gas resulting from incomplete combustion of gas in a gas fitting, but, to the extent that this regulation relates to such an escape or emission of carbon monoxide gas, the requirements imposed upon a supplier by paragraph (1) above shall, where the escape or emission is notified to the supplier by the person to whom gas has been supplied, be limited to advising that person of the immediate action to be taken to prevent such escape or emission and the need for the examination and, where necessary, repair of the fitting by a competent person.

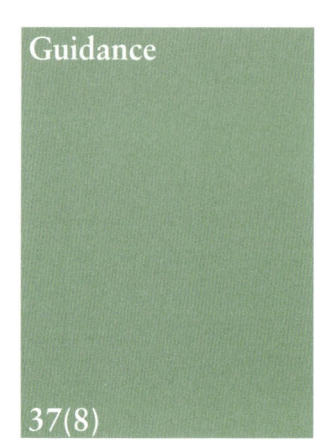

Guidance 37(8)

242 The requirements of regulation 37 apply both to an escape of fuel gas (other than any escape of natural gas from a 'network', as covered by the Gas Safety (Management) Regulations 1996), and to suspected or actual emissions of fumes, ie carbon monoxide from an appliance using gas (other than natural gas supplied from a 'network'). This means that requirements in regulation 37 extend to an emission, or suspected emission of carbon monoxide from any appliance using 'gas' as defined in regulation 2(1), eg LPG, apart from (in most cases) those using natural gas – see paragraph 241. However, the duty on gas suppliers in regulation 37(1) with regard to a report of CO escape/emission is restricted to providing advice on how to prevent the escape/emission (including identification of the faulty appliance/fitting (if possible) and action to isolate the gas supply) and on the need for examination, and where necessary, repair of the appliance/fitting by a competent person, eg a Gas Safe-registered engineer (see paragraph 230(c)–(d)).

Regulation 38 — Use of antifluctuators and valves

Regulation 38(1)–(4)

(1) Where a consumer uses gas for the purpose of working or supplying plant which is liable to produce pressure fluctuation in the gas supply such as to cause any danger to other consumers, he shall comply with such directions as may be given to him by the transporter of the gas to prevent such danger.

(2) Where a consumer intends to use for or in connection with the consumption of gas any gaseous substance he shall -

(a) give to the transporter of the gas at least 14 days notice in writing of that intention; and
(b) during such use comply with such directions as the transporter may have given to him to prevent the admission of such substance into the gas supply;

and in this paragraph "gaseous substance" includes compressed air but does not include any gaseous substance supplied by the transporter.

(3) Where a direction under paragraphs (1) or (2) above requires the provision of any device, the consumer shall ensure that the device is adequately maintained.

(4) Any direction given pursuant to this regulation shall be in writing.

Guidance

38(1)–(4)

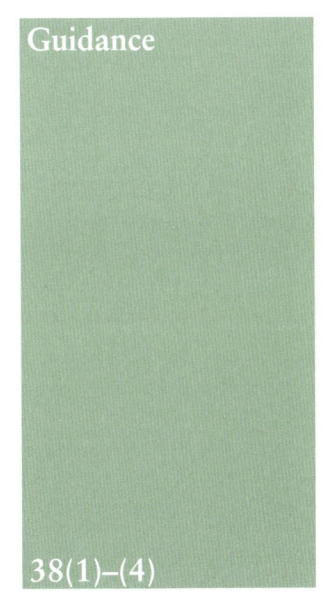

243 This regulation applies to consumers who use plant that may create pressure fluctuation in the gas supply (eg a compressor, engine or similar apparatus liable to produce a pressure below atmospheric in the gas main), or who intend to use in conjunction with gas another gaseous substance such as compressed air (for instance in gas/air mixing equipment or other process plant). The consumer should notify the gas transporter of intentions in either case (at least 14 days notice is specifically required under regulation 38(2)(a)), and is required to comply with directions given by the transporter for protection of the gas supply against possible pressure fluctuation, or introduction of extraneous gas, to prevent danger to other consumers. Any device, such as an antifluctuator, or non-return valve, specified by the gas transporter needs to be provided and maintained by the consumer.

244 Under Schedule 2B of the Gas Act 1986 (as inserted by the Gas Act 1995 and amended by these Regulations), the gas transporter may disconnect premises where a consumer fails to comply with requirements in regulation 38. The gas transporter is also empowered to disconnect, remove, test and replace any appliance/device required under this regulation, and to claim expenses from the consumer where the appliance is not found to be in proper order and repair.

Regulation 39

Exception as to liability

Regulation 39

No person shall be guilty of an offence by reason of contravention of regulation 3(2) or (6), 5(1), 7(3), 15, 16(2) or (3), 17(1), 27(5), 30 (insofar as it relates to the installation of a gas fire, other gas space heater or a gas water heater of more than 14 kilowatt gross heat input), 33(1), 35 or 36 of these Regulations in any case in which he can show that he took all reasonable steps to prevent that contravention.

Guidance

39

245 This regulation provides certain exceptions as to liability, under which a person is not deemed to be guilty of an offence, where they can show that they took all reasonable steps to prevent contravention of the provision concerned. This publication contains guidance in various areas, eg concerning access to premises to discharge landlord's duties under regulation 36 (eg see paragraph 213). However, it is finally for a court to decide whether 'all reasonable steps' have in fact been taken in particular circumstances, and whether a person is guilty of an offence.

246 The exceptions as to liability only apply to the particular provisions specified in regulation 39. It should be noted that they do not extend to the prohibition in regulation 30, concerning installation of certain instantaneous water heaters.

Regulation 40

Exemption certificates

Regulation

40(1)–(2)

(1) Subject to paragraph (2), the Health and Safety Executive may, by a certificate in writing, exempt any person or class of persons from any requirement or prohibition imposed by these Regulations, and any such exemption may be granted subject to conditions and to a limit of time and may be revoked at any time by a certificate in writing.

(2) The Health and Safety Executive shall not grant any such exemption unless, having regard to the circumstances of the case and in particular to -

(a) the conditions, if any, which it proposes to attach to the exemption; and
(b) any other requirements imposed by or under any enactment which apply to the case,

it is satisfied that the health and safety of persons likely to be affected by the exemption, will not be prejudiced in consequence of it.

Guidance

40(1)–(2)

247 This regulation enables HSE to grant exemptions. The intention is to use this power only in exceptional circumstances, such as to deal with circumstances (eg arising from technological change/innovation) which could not be foreseen when the Regulations were made.

248 Regulation 40(2) requires HSE to ensure that standards of health and safety will not be prejudiced by any exemption, so it is not sufficient for an application for exemption simply to assert that it is inconvenient or costly to comply. The applicant needs to explain carefully which particular provision cannot be observed and why, and the means by which an equivalent standard of health and safety is to be maintained.

Regulation 41

Revocation and amendments

Regulation 41

(1) The Gas Safety (Installation and Use) Regulations 1994[a], the Gas Safety (Installation and Use) (Amendment) Regulations 1996[b] and the Gas Safety (Installation and Use) (Amendment) (No. 2) Regulations 1996[c] are hereby revoked.

(2) Schedule 2B to the Gas Act 1986[d] shall be amended as follows -

(a) In paragraph 17(1) the words "pressure fluctuation in the transporter's pipe-line system and any other" and the words "or danger" shall be deleted;
(b) In paragraph 17(2) after the words "if so required" there shall be added "other than for the purpose of preventing danger"; and
(c) In paragraph 17(5) and (6) after the words "this paragraph" there shall be added "or regulation 38 of the Gas Safety (Installation and Use) Regulations 1998 or directions made thereunder".

(a) S.I. 1994/1886.
(b) S.I. 1996/550.
(c) S.I. 1996/2541.
(d) 1986 c. 44; Schedule 2B was inserted by the Gas Act 1995 (c.4 5) section 9(2) and Schedule 2.

Appendix 1

ACOP

Requirements for appliances and flues

1 This appendix summarises the main points that need to be addressed, as appropriate, in installation and other work, including safety checks, on gas appliances and flues. Additional matters may require attention in particular circumstances; reference should be made to appropriate standards, and Building Regulations where applicable, for further information.

(A) Appliances (regulations 26(1) and (9) and 35/36)

2 Gas installers carrying out installation or safety check work should ensure that:

(a) a sufficient permanent supply of air (by natural means) is available to the appliance for safe combustion of gas. Account needs to be taken of the size of the room, whether double-glazing is fitted, the location and size of air-bricks and other permanent air vents, and similar factors which could affect the adequacy of the air supply. It should be checked that vent openings are not obstructed;

(b) the room or space where the appliance is located is adequately ventilated, and that the means of ventilation is suitable;

(c) there are adequate and suitable means for removal of products of combustion from the appliance (see flue requirements in (B) below);

(d) the operating pressure and/or heat input of the appliance is correct. The installer should carry out the most appropriate test(s) for the appliance. This information is usually shown in manufacturer installation instructions or on the appliance data badge. In certain cases, eg when appliance burners are modified or replaced, such as for conversion from LPG to natural gas, it may be necessary to check both operating pressure and heat input;

(e) a visual check is made of the 'flame picture' (ie appearance) to ensure that it is satisfactory, or a measurement is made of combustion performance where appropriate;

(f) the appliance and associated gas fittings function safely, eg safety devices including flame protection, vitiation devices and fan proving systems operate satisfactorily;

(g) the gas soundness of the appliance is satisfactory;

(h) the appliance is physically stable, securely fitted and properly connected to other fittings.

(B) Flues (regulations 26, 27 and 35/36)

Domestic and other small scale flues

3 Dutyholders should ensure that:

(a) any flue is inspected and tested sufficiently to determine whether it is suitable and in a proper condition for safe operation of the appliance it is intended to serve. The detailed inspection arrangements necessary to ensure the requirements in (b)–(l) below are met will, to some extent, depend on the particular circumstances/equipment, and must be a matter for judgement by a competent gas installer. However, the following points should be noted:

  (i) wherever necessary, inspection/tests should be made with the appliance removed;

  (ii) in some cases, dismantling of equipment might be required, eg to establish continuity of a flue path in the heat exchanger of a central heating boiler where malfunction is suspected;

ACOP

(iii) suitable checks for gastightness should be made after any work is done on an appliance, including on installation pipework where this is disturbed directly or indirectly, for instance when an appliance is removed (eg see regulation 22(1));

(iv) any loftspace through which a flue passes should be examined, where necessary (for instance, during initial installation of an appliance and flue flow test, or subsequent maintenance/safety checks), to ascertain flue integrity through to the outside terminal – see paragraph 213 concerning access for inspection/testing;

(v) where access cannot be gained for inspection, such as where a flue runs partly through property not owned by the dutyholder (eg landlord) and access is refused by the occupant, all reasonable steps still need to be taken by the dutyholder to ensure overall flue integrity. This may involve making enquiries with occupants of property (including by 'recorded delivery' correspondance and personal contact as necessary) and requesting to see reports of examinations made by them or on their behalf. Where there are good reasons to suspect flueing problems, eg because of flue flow/spillage test failure (see (k) and (l) below) or clear medical evidence of carbon monoxide poisoning, it is essential to check the complete length of the flue; any associated appliance must not be used unless or until this is done;

(b) a flue is complete and continuous through its length, ie is undamaged and is adequately supported. A flue should not have intermediate openings, apart from:

(i) a draught stabiliser, balancing damper or relief opening which is in the same room, or space, as the appliance being served;

(ii) an opening for inspection or cleaning, which is fitted with a non-combustible gastight cover; or

(iii) an opening integral and essential to the correct operation of the flue, which is purpose-designed and properly located for its application, eg an opening in a vertex flue in an unoccupied loftspace (a guard should be fitted around such an opening, where necessary, to prevent possible ignition of nearby materials);

(c) more than one appliance is not connected to a flue, unless the flue has been specifically designed for this purpose;

(d) the effect of other open-flued appliances in the same room is properly taken into account. Where more than one such appliance is so installed, it should be ensured that:

(i) the heat output of the appliances is similar and that their flues terminate at the same height, preferably close together so that they are subject to the same wind conditions; and

(ii) flues are effective with all appliances in operation (see (k) and (l) below);

(e) the terminal is correctly sited; this should include adequate separation from any site boundary to ensure that the flue will continue to function safely and emissions will not present a hazard to any person either on the site concerned or in adjoining property, including in the event of any future building development on adjoining premises (which might extend close or up to the site boundary);

(f) any chimney has not been closed over/modified so as to interfere with flue operation. Any flue damper or restrictor plates should be removed or permanently fixed open, to avoid obstructing the flue;

(g) any debris, eg in a fire/catchment space, is removed before installing/ re-installing an appliance, that the catchment space is of adequate size and

Appendix 1

ACOP

that any openings within this space (other than those for the appliance connection and flue) are effectively sealed. Flues and chimneys previously used for oil or solid fuel appliances need to be swept before being used with a gas appliance;

(h) where a masonry flue or its liner seems to be in a poor condition, thorough examination is carried out to determine whether it is safe for continued use. Renovation should be carried out, where necessary, and consideration given to fitting (correctly sized) metal flue liners; in certain cases, liners are required under Building Regulations;

(i) where components, such as external sections of flues (eg terminals), metal flue liners and inspection openings show signs of damage, eg corrosion, they are replaced as necessary. When replacing an appliance connected to a chimney lined with a metallic liner, the existing liner should normally be replaced unless it is considered suitable for safe operation throughout the lifespan of the new appliance;

(j) when flue liners are fitted or replaced, the flue is tested to ensure it is operating satisfactorily (see (k) and (l), below);

(k) a flue flow test is carried out to check the effectiveness of the flue and ensure that there is no leakage into another part of the premises (including any loft) or, as appropriate, other adjoining premises. (This is particularly important where a number of chimneys combine into a multiple chimney stack.) Smoke coming out of other than the correct terminal, or a down-draught or no-flow condition, indicates an unsatisfactory flue;

(l) after completion of a satisfactory flue flow test, a smoke spillage test is carried out, with the appliance connected and operating, to check that the products of combustion are being safely removed. The test should be conducted in accordance with the appliance manufacturer instructions, and take into account any factors which may adversely affect flue efficiency, eg operation of extractor fans or forced air heating systems in the room housing the appliance or any adjoining room (with interconnecting doors open).

Larger commercial flues

4   Larger commercial (and industrial) premises often have purpose-designed flue systems. The appliance designer/manufacturer instructions need to be followed when installing, servicing and maintaining such systems. The instructions may well stipulate a particular commissioning procedure to be followed. Reference should also be made to appropriate standards.

Appendix 1

Appendix 2 — Examples of potentially unsafe situations (regulation 34)

Guidance

1 This appendix gives some examples of situations which might lead to a gas appliance being considered 'dangerous' in terms of regulation 34. However, these examples are only intended to provide a general illustration of potentially unsafe situations; the level of risk, and whether a gas appliance is in fact 'unsafe' in any particular case, must be a matter for judgement by a competent person, eg a gas engineer who is, or is employed by, a member of a class of persons approved by HSE under regulation 3 (see paragraphs 198–200).

2 Every situation described below will not necessarily lead to a gas appliance being 'dangerous', in practice. In some cases, danger will be clear, such as where gas is escaping or there is a high risk of this happening (eg open-ended pipes connected to gas supply), gas appliance safety devices (flame protection etc) are inoperative, or where there are clear signs of products of combustion being emitted into occupied areas (and there is no evidence to show that the problem has been corrected). However, in most situations, the level of risk will largely depend on the individual circumstances, which need to be taken into account in any assessment. In case of doubt, the responsible person/gas engineer should seek further advice, for instance by consulting industry guidance on 'unsafe situations' procedures; or contacting the emergency gas service, ie for LPG, the gas supplier, or in any other case (including natural gas) the Gas Emergency Freephone Number 0800 111 999.

3 The causal factors specified below serve both to indicate features which may contribute to the overall risk in a particular case, and areas which might need to be addressed in associated remedial action. This information (structured under hazards specified in ACOP paragraph 198) is not exhaustive and situations outside the scope of the Regulations, eg involving gas service pipes, are excluded.

(1) Incomplete combustion of gas

4 This includes any case where there is clear evidence of incomplete combustion (eg from flame appearance, sooting, or combustion analysis), leading to dangerous emissions of products of combustion into an occupied area, eg as evidenced from medically confirmed reports of ill health from users. The potential risk is primarily related to flueless and open-flued appliances and is likely to be most pronounced where they are located in confined/poorly ventilated rooms or compartments (see also (2) and (3) below). It should be noted that certain gas appliances, eg some 'living flame' effect fires, are specifically designed to operate safely using incomplete combustion.

5 Factors which may lead to insufficient air being available for complete combustion to take place include:

(a) inadequate or defective ventilation of the room/area in which the appliance is located, eg air bricks/louvres of insufficient size or number, or vent openings obstructed;
(b) malfunction or failure of fan(s) supplying combustion air to an appliance, eg where an airflow proving device is not fitted, or is defective.

(2) Removal of products of combustion not being safely carried out

6 This includes any case where there are clear signs/evidence of significant spillage of combustion products into an occupied area, eg from appliance/flue function tests, air sampling or medically confirmed reports of ill effects on users.

7   Factors which may inhibit safe removal of combustion products include where:

(a) design or construction of a flue/chimney is defective, eg flue size is insufficient for the application, or the routing of the flue or position of the termination is incorrect, such as with a wall facing/adjacent termination. Obstruction and inadequate removal/dispersal of combustion products may result, for instance, from the proximity of a building on the site where the appliance is installed, or a structure within neighbouring property where a safe separation distance has not been provided between the flue termination and site boundary (see below and regulation 27);

(b) a flue is obstructed, eg with soot from previous use with an oil/solid fuel fired appliance or debris (for instance, from an unlined masonry/brick flue). Accumulation of debris in, or the absence of, a catchment space may be an indicator of a potential risk;

(c) a flue is incomplete or damaged, eg as a result of not being adequately supported, or discharges within a building, eg a loftspace;

(d) a manual flue damper is fixed, other than in the open position;

(e) the efficiency of a flue is adversely affected by ventilation arrangements, eg operation of extractor fans in the room housing the appliance, or an adjoining room (with interconnecting doors open);

(f) a flueless or open-flued appliance is installed in a confined/poorly ventilated room (see also (1) and (3), and prohibitions in regulation 30 on the installation of certain gas appliances in specified locations);

(g) more than one appliance is connected to the same flue, and the flue is not designed for this purpose, and/or the appliances fitted to the flue are in separate rooms ventilated from different sides of the building;

(h) there is another gas, oil or solid fuel appliance in the same, or closely adjoining room, which has a higher flue or the terminal is located on a different part of the roof. The action of the other flue may cause spillage of combustion products; or

(i) there is an open solid fuel fire in the same, or closely adjoining room. The action of the solid fuel fire may cause spillage of combustion products.

(3) Insufficient oxygen available for the occupants of the room/space in which the appliance is fitted

8   This includes any case where there is clear evidence that ventilation is insufficient, eg from results of air tests for carbon monoxide/oxygen, and/or medically confirmed reports of ill effects on people in the room or space housing the appliance. In practice, the risk will normally coincide with cases where there is insufficient air for proper combustion (see (1), above); it mainly relates to flueless, open-flued, and other appliances where the combustion air supply is drawn from the room or space housing the appliance.

9   Factors which may lead to insufficient ventilation include where:

(a) ventilation openings, eg airbricks and louvres, are of inadequate size/number, or they are not properly located, eg leading to 'dead areas'. This includes where installation of a gas appliance of increased capacity has not been matched by a required increase in air supply;

(b) ventilation openings are obstructed, eg where airbricks are blocked or adjustable louvres/fly screens have been fitted (in contravention of standards) and closed to conserve heat; or

(c) an appliance has too high a heat input for the room in which it is installed.

(4) Gas leakage

10 This includes any gas leakage (where there is a smell of gas), arising for example from the use of unsatisfactory materials, bad workmanship or lack of maintenance (see also appropriate standards and regulation 37).

11 Examples of situations where gas escape may or may be likely to occur include where:

(a) an open-ended pipe has been left connected to a gas supply, ie without being sealed off (eg see regulation 22);
(b) pipework is liable to fail, eg as a result of mechanical or corrosion damage; or
(c) an inappropriate design, construction, or material has been used for the particular application (such as a flexible connection made of garden hose).

(5) Other danger

12 This may include situations where:

(a) a primary meter is seriously malfunctioning, eg as a result of mechanical or other damage such as from fire exposure or contact with electrical equipment;
(b) no means is provided for safe regulation of the gas supply pressure (eg see regulation 14);
(c) an appliance malfunctions, eg due to lack of maintenance or incorrect assembly, so as to cause it to 'burn back';
(d) an appliance is installed too close to combustible material, giving rise to a risk of ignition/fire, eg a gas fire with burners an insufficient distance above a carpet (evidence of scorching may be an indicator);
(e) an appliance is unsuitable for use with the gas supplied;
(f) an appliance is dangerously insecure/unstable;
(g) appliance safety devices, eg flame failure devices, are inoperative or have been deliberately defeated;
(h) more than one appliance is fitted to a 'common' flue and either, or both, of the appliance(s) are not fitted with flame failure devices (see also comments under (2) above); or
(i) controls on a sealed central heating/water heating system are defective, giving rise to a steam explosion risk.

Appendix 3

Guidance

Summary of legislation

(Note: this appendix does not form part of the Code.)

HSE legislation

Health and Safety at Work etc Act 1974 (HSW Act)

1   This Act applies to everyone concerned with work activities, ranging from employers, self-employed, and employees, to manufacturers, designers, suppliers and importers of materials for use at work, and people in control of premises. It also includes provisions to protect members of the public. The duties apply both to individual people and to corporations, companies, partnerships, local authorities, nationalised industries etc. The duties are expressed in general terms, so that they apply to all types of work activity and work situations. Every employer has a duty to ensure, so far as is reasonably practicable, the health, safety and welfare at work of his or her employees. The principles of safety responsibility and safe working are expressed in sections 2–9. Employers and self-employed are required to carry out their undertakings in such a way as to ensure, so far as is reasonably practicable, that they do not expose people who are not their employees to risks to their health and safety (sections 3(1) and 3(2)). In some areas the general duties have been supplemented by specific requirements in Regulations made under the Act and such Regulations will continue to be made. Specific legal requirements are also included in earlier legislation which is still in force. Failure to comply with the general requirements of the Act, or specific requirements found elsewhere may result in legal proceedings.

2   Although some of the duties imposed by the Act and related legislation are absolute, many are qualified by the words 'so far as is reasonably practicable' or 'so far as is practicable'. If someone is prosecuted for failing to comply with a duty which is qualified by these words, it is up to the accused to show to the court that it was not reasonably practicable or practicable, as appropriate, for him/her to do more than was done to comply with the duty.

3   The judgement of what is reasonably practicable means weighing up the seriousness of the risk against the difficulty and cost of removing it.

4   Where the difficulty and cost are high and a careful assessment of the risk shows it to be insignificant, action may not be necessary although in some cases there are things that have to be done at all costs. No allowance is made for size, nature or profitability of a business.

5   Sections 21–23 provide for improvement and prohibition notices to be issued; section 33 provides for prosecution and penalties; section 15 provides for Regulations to be made; sections 16 and 17 provide for Codes of Practice to be approved, and for their use in legal proceedings.

Pipelines Safety Regulations 1996 (PSR)

6   These Regulations impose requirements on pipelines for purposes of health and safety. The requirements, with certain exceptions, cover any pipe or system of pipes for conveying fluids; this includes pipes supplying gas to premises (ie transmission pipes, distribution mains and service pipes) but excludes anything downstream of an emergency control (eg installation pipework, meters and other fittings, as covered by GSIUR). Any pipeline contained wholly within the premises occupied by a single undertaking, or contained wholly within a caravan site, is not covered by the Regulations.

7   The Regulations include requirements for design, construction, installation, examination and maintenance of pipelines, and for decommissioning of disused pipelines. Additional requirements are imposed in relation to certain ('major accident hazard') pipelines, including notification to HSE of specified information, preparation of a major accident prevention document and drawing up emergency procedures.

Gas Safety (Management) Regulations 1996 (as amended) (GSMR)

8   These Regulations deal with the management of the safe flow of gas (defined as any substance in a gaseous state which consists wholly or mainly of methane), whether in a single system or a network of connected systems. The Regulations make it unlawful for gas to be conveyed in a system or network without a safety case being prepared by the conveyor and accepted by HSE. Where two or more gas transporters operate on a network, there has to be a sole network emergency co-ordinator (NEC) for that network, whose safety case has been accepted by HSE.

9   The Regulations cover requirements for emergency response to and investigation of gas escapes. These requirements apply to an escape of natural gas, or actual/suspected emission of carbon monoxide (CO) from an appliance using natural gas; they interface with GSIUR provisions on escapes of other fuel gases and emissions of CO from appliances using gases other than natural gas.

10   Requirements for the content and other characteristics of gas conveyed in a network are also included. For example, maximum quantities of hydrogen, oxygen, hydrogen sulphide, sulphur and other impurities are specified. Although GSIUR does not cover gases wholly or mainly comprising hydrogen when used in non-domestic premises, a gas containing the 0.1% molar (approximately 0.2%) maximum level allowed under the GSMR is covered generally under GSIUR (see definition of 'gas' in regulation 2(1)).

Workplace (Health, Safety and Welfare) Regulations 1992 (WHSR)

11   These Regulations impose requirements with respect to the health, safety and welfare or persons in a 'workplace' which, with certain exceptions, covers any premises or part of premises which are not domestic premises and are made available to any person as a place of work. This includes certain areas, eg staircases, lobbies and corridors used as a means of access to, or egress from a workplace or where facilities are provided for use in connection with the workplace, eg boiler/central heating plant rooms.

12   The Regulations include requirements for maintenance of the workplace and certain equipment, devices and systems; ventilation; temperature; lighting; cleanliness, and other provisions. These requirements are imposed on employers, persons who have, to any extent, control of a workplace, and certain others.

Management of Health and Safety at Work Regulations 1999 (MHSWR)

13   The central feature of these Regulations is the duty imposed on employers and self-employed persons to make a suitable and sufficient assessment of risks to the health and safety of employees, and non-employees affected by their work. This links closely with specific duties, eg on gas installers and suppliers, under GSIUR (see under 'Interface with other health and safety legislation' in the Introduction to this ACOP). MHSWR also requires effective planning and review of protective measures (which include those to comply with GSIUR), health surveillance, emergency procedures, information and training.

Provision and Use of Work Equipment Regulations 1998 (PUWER)

14   These Regulations impose health and safety requirements with respect to 'work equipment', which includes any machinery, appliance, apparatus or tool and certain assemblies of components (this would include certain gas appliances/fittings). The requirements address the suitability of work equipment; maintenance and associated records; inspection and associated records; measures to deal with specific risks (including use of designated persons to operate, repair, maintain and service equipment); information, instruction and training of users and others; and other specific areas (eg dangerous parts of machinery, protection from high and low temperature, lighting and stability of equipment).

15   The requirements apply to employers in respect of work equipment provided for, or used by, their employees for use at work. They also apply to self-employed persons and persons in control of work equipment to any extent.

Construction (Design and Management) Regulations 2007 (CDM)

16   These Regulations place wide-ranging duties on clients, designers, planning supervisors and contractors to take health and safety matters into account and manage them effectively from the planning stages of a construction project through commission and any future construction work, including dismantling or demolition.

Pressure Systems Safety Regulations 2000 (PSSR)

17   The aim of these Regulations is to prevent serious injury from the hazard of stored energy, as a result of the failure of a pressure system, or one of its component parts. They are concerned with steam at any pressure, gases which exert a pressure in excess of 0.5 bar above atmospheric pressure and fluids which may exert a pressure in excess of 0.5 bar above atmospheric (gauge) pressure. Exceptionally, pipelines are within scope when used to convey gases and liquefied gases above 2 bar gauge. Pipelines include: compressors; valves; associated pipework; and other apparatus used to cause the gas to flow through the pipeline system; the primary shut-off valve at each end of the pipeline and the pipeline protective devices. This guidance should be read in conjunction with the publication *A guide to the Pipelines Safety Regulations 1996* (see Appendix 4).

18   PSSR place duties on designers, maufacturers, importers, suppliers, installers and users (or owners in the case of mobile systems) of pressure systems. The Regulations also place certain duties on Competent Persons. The requirements for design, manufacture, supply, and certain marking and information requirements, do not apply to equipment and assemblies supplied in accordance with the Pressure Equipment Regulations 1999.

19   PSSR also apply to pressure systems where a transportable pressure receptacle (gas cylinder) is connected. The requirements for the design, manufacture, supply, and periodic inspection of the gas cylinder is covered by the Carriage of Dangerous Goods and Use of Transportable Pressure Equipment Regulations 2007.

Health and Safety (Safety Signs and Signals) Regulations 1996 (SSR)

20   These Regulations implement an EC Directive on the minimum requirements for the provision of safety and/or health signs at work. Under these Regulations, safety signs complying with specified descriptions must be provided where the risk assessment made under regulation 3 of the Management of Health and Safety at Work Regulations 1999 indicates that (residual) risks cannot be avoided or controlled in other ways. Although certain requirements apply to signs concerning storage and piping of hazardous substances, exclusions are provided for signs used in relation to the supply of equipment or substances, for transport of dangerous goods and for regulation of transport (eg as covered by separate legal provisions).

21   The Regulations also include requirements in relation to the instruction and training of employees in the meaning of safety signs and the measures to be taken in respect of such signs. SSR does not apply to self-employed persons or to premises which are not workplaces, but similar requirements might be necessary in these situations to meet general obligations under the Health and Safety at Work etc Act 1974.

Dangerous Substances and Explosive Atmospheres Regulations 2002 (DSEAR)

22   These Regulations impose requirements for the purpose of eliminating or reducing risks to safety from fire, explosion or other events arising from the hazardous properties of a 'dangerous substance' in connection with work. This includes flammable gases, such as natural gas, propane and butane.

23   The Regulations include a requirement for employers to carry out a suitable and sufficient risk assessment of risks to employees, where a dangerous substance is or may be present at the workplace and to eliminate or reduce the risk so far as is reasonably practicable. This builds on the related duty to carry out a general risk assessment under the Management of Health and Safety at Work Regulations 1999.

24   Places at the workplace where explosive atmospheres may occur must be classified as hazardous or non-hazardous, hazardous places are required to be classified into zones based on the frequency and duration of the occurrence of an explosive atmosphere and equipment and protective systems in hazardous places need to comply with specified requirements. These particular requirements generally do not apply to gas appliances as defined in the Gas Safety (Installation and Use) Regulations, or to other gas fittings located in domestic premises. However, they do apply to certain situations within these Regulations, eg work at commercial premises, and to service pipes generally.

Reporting of Injuries, Diseases and Dangerous Occurrences Regulations 1995 (RIDDOR)

25   These Regulations require employers to report specified occupational injuries, diseases and dangerous events to HSE. Certain gas incidents are reportable by suppliers of gas through fixed pipe distribution systems/LPG suppliers, and gas installers are required to report certain dangerous gas appliances to HSE.

Other legislation

Gas Acts 1986 and 1995 (GA)

26 The Gas Act 1995 updated provisions in the Gas Act 1986, including new licensing arrangements for public gas transporters and permitting competition in the domestic gas market.

27 A number of safety issues are both directly and indirectly addressed, including detailed provisions (some new), inserted into the Gas Act 1986 (under Schedule 2B – the 'gas code') by the 1995 Act – GA 1995 Schedule 2 refers. These provisions include duties to notify connection/disconnection of service pipes, and disconnection of meters in certain circumstances; maintenance of service pipes; duties on public gas transporters in relation to certain gas escapes, and entry powers in specified circumstances. Safety provisions concerning antifluctuators and valves (previously included in section 17 of the 'gas code') were revoked by GSIUR and are now covered by these Regulations (regulation 38 refers).

Gas Appliances (Safety) Regulations 1995 (GASR)

28 These Regulations, which implement an EC Directive on gas appliances, require appliances and fittings to which they apply to conform with specified essential requirements and to be safe when normally used. Supply of these products is prohibited unless they bear the CE Marking and safety is underpinned by valid certification/declaration of conformity. The Regulations include detailed procedures for product conformity attestation by third-party notified bodies, appointed by the Secretary of State.

29 The Regulations also specify requirements for information to be provided with new gas appliances, eg covering safe installation, operation and maintenance.

Building Regulations and Building Standards (Scotland) Regulations

30 Building Regulations address various aspects of building design/construction, including health and safety, energy conservation and the welfare and convenience of disabled people.

31 A number of documents have been approved by the Secretary of State under the Building Regulations as practical (non-mandatory) guidance to meeting requirements under the Regulations, including on ventilation and heat producing (eg certain gas) appliances. The Approved Documents cover the more common building situations but alternative ways of demonstrating compliance may be appropriate in other circumstances. In case of legal action, following the guidance may be used as evidence to demonstrate compliance with the Regulations.

32 Similar 'deemed to satisfy' guidance is provided in technical standards of the Building Standards (Scotland) Regulations. This includes heat producing installations and storage of liquid and gas fuels (Part F) and ventilation of buildings (Part K).

Appendix 4

Appropriate standards, ACOPs, guidance and relevant information sources

Guidance

The publications listed below were current when this ACOP/guidance was first published but the list should be taken to refer to any subsequent amendments or latest editions.

Appropriate standards

The following British Standards (listed under subject area) are regarded as 'appropriate standards' for the purpose of this ACOP/guidance – see the explanatory note in the Introduction to this publication. The list is not comprehensive and is subject to change as standards are revised and new standards introduced.

Terminology

BS 1179-6:1980 *Glossary of terms used in the gas industry. Combustion and utilisation, including installation at consumers' premises*

Ventilation

BS 493:1995 *Specification for airbricks and gratings for wall ventilation*

BS 5440-2:2009 *Flueing and ventilation for gas appliances of rated input not exceeding 70 kW net (1st, 2nd and 3rd family gases). Specification for the installation and maintenance of ventilation provision for gas appliances*

BS 5925:1991 *Code of practice for ventilation principles and designing for natural ventilation*

BS EN 721:2004 *Leisure accommodation vehicles. Safety ventilation requirements*

Flues

BS 41:1973 *Specification for cast iron spigot and socket flue or smoke pipes and fittings*

BS 567:1973 *Specification for asbestos-cement flue pipes and fittings, light quality*

BS 715:2005 *Specification for metal flue boxes for gas-fired appliances not exceeding 20 kW*

BS EN 1856-1:2009 *Chimneys. Requirements for metal chimneys. System chimney products*

BS EN 1856-2:2009 *Chimneys. Requirements for metal chimneys. Metal flue liners and connecting flue pipes*

BS 835:1973 *Specification for asbestos-cement flue pipes and fittings, heavy quality*

BS EN 13502:2002 *Chimneys. Requirements and test methods for clay/ceramic flue terminals*

BS EN 1858:2008 *Chimneys. Components. Concrete flue blocks*

BS EN 1806:2006 *Chimneys. Clay/ceramic flue blocks for single wall chimneys Requirements and test methods*

BS EN 1859:2000 *Chimneys. Metal chimneys. Test methods*

BS 5440-1:2008 *Flueing and ventilation for gas appliances of rated heat input not exceeding 70 kW net (1st, 2nd and 3rd family gases). Specification for the installation and maintenance of ventilation provision for gas appliances*

BS 5440-2:2009 *Flueing and ventilation for gas appliances of rated heat input not exceeding 70 kW net (1st, 2nd and 3rd family gases). Specification for the installation and maintenance of ventilation provision for gas appliances*

BS 5854:1980 *Code of practice for flues and flue structures in buildings*

BS EN 1857:2010 *Chimneys. Components. Concrete flue liners*

Installation

BS EN 1775:2007 *Gas supply. Gas pipework for buildings. Maximum operating pressure less than or equal to 5 bar. Functional recommendations*

BS 5482-1:2005 *Code of practice for domestic butane- and propane-gas-burning installations. Installations at permanent dwellings, residential park homes and commercial premises, with installation pipework sizes not exceeding DN 25 for steel and DN 28 for corrugated stainless steel or copper*

BS 5482-2:1977 *Domestic butane- and propane-gas-burning installations. Installations in caravans and non-permanent dwellings*

PD 5482-3:2005 *Code of practice for domestic butane and propane gas-burning installations. Installations in boats, yachts and other vessels*

BS EN ISO 10239:2008 *Small craft. Liquefied petroleum gas (LPG) systems*

BS 5546:2010 *Specification for installation and maintenance of gas-fired water-heating appliances of rated input not exceeding 70 kW net*

BS 5864:2004 *Installation and maintenance of gas-fired ducted air heaters of rated input not exceeding 70 kW net (2nd and 3rd family gases). Specification*

BS 5871 *Specification for the installation and maintenance of gas fires, convector heaters, fire/back boilers and decorative fuel effect gas appliances*
Part 1:2005 *Gas fires, convector heaters, fire/back boilers and heating stoves (2nd and 3rd family gases)*
Part 2:2005 *Inset live fuel effect gas fires of heat input not exceeding 15 kW, and fire/back boilers (2nd and 3rd family gases)*
Part 3:2005 *Decorative fuel effect gas appliances of heat input not exceeding 20 kW (2nd and 3rd family gases)*
Part 4:2007 *Independent gas-fired flueless fires convector heaters and heating stoves of nominal heat input not exceeding 6 kW (2nd and 3rd family gases)*

BS 6172:2004 *Installation and maintenance of domestic gas cooking appliance (2nd and 3rd family gases)*

BS 6173:2009 *Specification for installation of gas-fired catering appliances for use in all types of catering establishments (2nd and 3rd family gases)*

BS 6230:2005 *Specification for installation of gas-fired forced convection air heaters for commercial and industrial space heating (2nd and 3rd family gases)*

BS 6400:2006 *Specification for installation, exchange, relocation and removal of gas meters with a maximum capacity not exceeding 6m^3/h.*

BS 6400-1:2006 *Specification for installation, exchange, relocation and removal of gas meters with a maximum capacity not exceeding 6m^3/h. Low pressure (2nd family gases)*

BS 6400-2:2006 *Specification for installation, exchange, relocation and removal of gas meters with a maximum capacity not exceeding 6 m^3/h. Medium pressure (2nd family gases)*

BS 6400-3:2007 *Specification for installation, exchange, relocation and removal of gas meters with a maximum capacity not exceeding 6m^3/h. Low and medium pressure (3rd family gases)*

BS 6644:2005 + A1:2008 *Specification for installation of gas-fired hot water boilers of rated inputs between 70 kW (net) and 1.8 MW (net) (2nd and 3rd family gases)*

BS 6798:2009 *Specification for installation and maintenance of gas-fired boilers of rated input not exceeding 70 kW net*

BS 6891:2005 + A2:2008 *Installation of low pressure gas pipework of up to 35 mm (R1 $^1/_4$) in domestic premises (2nd family gas). Specification*

BS EN 15287-1:2007 *Chimneys. Design, installation and commissioning of chimneys. Chimneys for non room-sealed heating appliances*

BS 7624:2004 *Installation and maintenance of domestic direct gas-fired tumble dryers of up to 6 kW heat input (2nd and 3rd family gases). Specification*

Valves, meters and regulators (governors)

BS EN 88-1:2007 *Pressure regulators and associated safety devices for gas appliances. Pressure regulators for inlet pressures up to and including 500 mbar*

BS EN 161:2007 *Automatic shut-off valves for gas burners and gas appliances*

BS 1552:1995 *Specification for open bottomed taper plug valves for 1st, 2nd and 3rd family gases up to 200 mbar*

BS EN 13785:2005 + A1:2008 *Regulators with a capacity of up to and including 100 kg/h, having a maximum nominal outlet pressure of up to and including 4 bar, other than those covered by EN 12864 and their associated safety devices for butane, propane or their mixtures*

BS EN 13786:2004 + A1:2008 *Automatic change-over valves having a maximum outlet pressure of up to and including 4 bar with a capacity of up to and including 100 kg/h, and their associated safety devices for butane, propane or their mixtures*

BS EN 12864:2001 + A3:2009 *Low-pressure, non adjustable regulators having a maximum outlet pressure of less than or equal to 200 mbar, with a capacity of less than or equal to 4 kg/h, and their associated safety devices for butane, propane or their mixtures*

BS 6448:1995 *Specification for gas appliance governors of DN greater than 50 and for inlet pressures up to 200 mbar*

BS 15287-1:2007 *Chimneys. Design, installation and commissioning of chimneys. Chimneys for non-roomsealed heating appliances*

BS 7461:1991 *Specification for electrically operated automatic gas shut-off valves fitted with throughput adjusters, proof of closure switches, closed position indicator switches or gas flow control*

BS EN 12405-1:2005 *Gas meters. Conversion devices. Volume conversion*

BS EN 1359:1999 *Gas meters. Diaphragm gas meters*

BS EN 12261:2002 *Gas meters. Turbine gas meters*

BS EN 12480:2002 *Gas meters. Rotary displacement gas meters*

Tubing

BS 669 *Flexible hoses, end fittings and sockets for gas burning appliances.*
Part 1:1989 *Specification for strip-wound metallic flexible hoses, covers, end fittings and sockets for domestic appliances burning 1st and 2nd family gases*
Part 2:1997 *Specification for corrugated metallic flexible hoses, covers, end fittings and sockets for catering appliances burning 1st, 2nd and 3rd family gases*
BS 2775:1987 *Specification for rubber stoppers and tubing for general laboratory use*

BS 3212:1991 *Specification for flexible rubber tubing, rubber hose, and rubber hose assemblies for use in LPG vapour phase and LPG/air installations*

BS 4089:1999 *Specification for metallic hose assemblies for liquid petroleum gases and liquefied natural gases*

BS 6501-1:2004 *Metal hose assemblies. Guidance on the construction and use of corrugated hose assemblies*

BS EN ISO 10380:2003 *Pipework. Corrugated metal hoses and hose assemblies*

BS EN 1762:2003 *Rubber hoses and hose assemblies for liquefied petroleum gas, LPG (liquid or gaseous phase), and natural gas up to 25 bar (2,5 MPa). Specification*

Appliances

BS EN 203-1:2005 + A1:2008 *Gas heated catering equipment. General safety rules*

BS EN 297:1994 *Gas-fired central heating boilers. Type B11 and B11BS boilers fitted with atmospheric burners of nominal heat input not exceeding 70 kW*

BS EN 625:1996 *Gas-fired central heating boilers. Specific requirements for domestic hot water operation of combination boilers of nominal heat input not exceeding 70 kW*

BS EN 676:2003 + A2:2008 *Automatic forced draught burners for gaseous fuels*

BS 5991:2006 *Specification for indirect gas fired forced convection air heaters with rated heat inputs greater than 330 kW but not exceeding 2 MW for industrial and commercial space heating. Safety and performance requirements (excluding electrical requirements) (2nd family gases)*

BS EN 416-1:2009 *Single burner gas-fired overhead radiant-tube heaters for non-domestic use. Safety*

BS EN 419-1:2009 *Non-domestic gas-fired overhead luminous radiant heaters. Safety*

BS 5258 *Safety of domestic gas appliances*
Part 1:1986 *Specification for central heating boilers and circulators*
Part 9:1989 *Specification for combined appliances: fanned-circulation ducted-air heaters/circulators*

BS 7977-1:2009 *Specification for safety and rational use of energy of domestic gas appliances. Radiant convectors*

BS 7977-2:2003 *Specification for safety and rational use of energy of domestic gas appliances. Combined appliances. Gas fire/back boiler*

BS EN 1266:2002 *Independent gas fired convection heaters incorporating a fan to assist transportation of combustion air and/or flue gases*

BS EN 30-1-3:2003 *Domestic cooking appliances burning gas. Safety. Appliances having a glass ceramic hotplate*

BS EN 483:1999 + A4:2007 *Gas-fired central heating boilers. Type C boilers of nominal heat input not exceeding 70 kW*

BS EN 732:1999 *Specifications for dedicated liquefied petroleum gas appliances. Absorption refrigerators*

BS EN 89:2000 *Gas-fired storage water heaters for the production of domestic hot water*

BS EN 449:2002 + A1:2007 *Specification for dedicated liquefied petroleum gas appliances. Domestic flueless space heaters (including diffusive catalytic combustion heaters)*

BS EN 509:2000 *Decorative fuel-effect gas appliances*

BS 5809:1980 *Specification for safety and efficiency of the gas heating equipment of commercial dishwashing machines*

BS 5885 *Automatic gas burners*
Part 1:1988 *Specification for burners with input rating 60 kW and above*
Part 2:1987 *Specification for packaged burners with input rating 7.5 kW up to but excluding 60 kW*

BS 5978 *Safety and performance of gas-fired hot water boilers (60 kW to 2 MW input)*
Part 1:1989 *Specification for general requirements*
Part 2:1989 *Specification for additional requirements for boilers with atmospheric burners*
Part 3:1989 *Specification for additional requirements for boilers with forced or induced draught burners*

BS EN 656:2000 *Gas-fired central heating boilers. Type B boilers of nominal heat input exceeding 70 kW but not exceeding 300 kW*

BS 5986:1980 *Specification for electrical safety and performance of gas-fired space heating appliances with inputs 60 kW to 2 MW*

BS 5990:2006 *Specification for direct gas-fired forced convection air heaters with rated heat inputs greater than 330 kW but not exceeding 2 MW for industrial and commercial space heating. Safety and performance requirements (excluding electrical requirements) (2nd family gases)*

BS EN 525:2009 *Non-domestic direct gas-fired forced convection air heaters for space heating not exceeding a net heat input of 300 kW*

BS 6896:2005 *Specification for installation of gas-fired overhead radiant heaters for industrial and commercial heating (2nd and 3rd family gases)*

BS EN 13410:2001 *Gas-fired overhead radiant heaters. Ventilation requirements for non-domestic premises*

BS EN 461:1999 *Specification for dedicated liquefied petroleum gas appliances. Flueless non-domestic space heaters not exceeding 10 kW*

BS 7462:1991 *Specification for electrical safety of domestic gas appliances*

BS EN 60335-2-102:2006 + A1:2010 *Household and similar electrical appliances. Safety. Particular requirements for gas, oil and solid-fuel burning appliances having electrical connections*

BS EN 1596:1998 *Specification for liquefied petroleum gas appliances. Mobile and portable non-domestic forced convection direct fired air heaters*

BS EN 778:2009 *Domestic gas-fired forced convection air heaters for space heating not exceeding a net heat input of 70 kW, without a fan to assist transportation of combustion air and/or combustion products*

BS EN 498:1998 *Specification for dedicated liquefied petroleum gas appliances. Barbecues for outdoor use*

BS EN 26:1998 *Gas-fired instantaneous water heaters for the production of domestic hot water, fitted with atmospheric burners*

BS EN 30-1-1:2008 *Domestic cooking appliances burning gas. Safety. General*

BS EN 30-1-2:1999 *Domestic cooking appliances burning gas. Safety. Appliances having forced-convection ovens and/or grills*

BS EN 30-1-3:2003 *Domestic cooking appliances burning gas. Safety. Appliances having a glass ceramic hotplate*

BS EN 30-2-1:1998 *Domestic cooking appliances burning gas. Rational use of energy. General*

BS EN 30-2-2:1999 *Domestic cooking appliances burning gas. Rational use of energy. Appliances having forced-convection ovens and/or grills*

General

BS 476-22:1987 *Fire tests on building materials and structures. Methods for determination of the fire resistance of non-loadbearing elements of construction*

BS 1710:1984 *Specification for identification of pipelines and services*

BS 8313:1997 *Code of practice for accommodation of building services in ducts*

British Standards can be obtained in PDF or hard copy formats from BSI: http://shop.bsigroup.com or by contacting BSI Customer Services for hard copies only Tel: 020 8996 9001 email: cservices@bsigroup.com.

HSE Approved Codes of Practice

HSE publications are available for free download at www.hse.gov.uk

Standards of training in safe gas installation. Approved Code of Practice COP20 HSE Books 1987 ISBN 978 0 7176 0603 0

Managing health and safety in construction: Construction (Design and Management) Regulations 2007. Approved Code of Practice L144 HSE Books 2007 ISBN 978 0 7176 6223 4

Design, construction and installation of gas service pipes. Pipelines Safety Regulations 1996. Approved Code of Practice and guidance L81 HSE Books 1996 ISBN 978 0 7176 1172 0

Management of health and safety at work. Management of Health and Safety at Work Regulations 1999. Approved Code of Practice and guidance L21 (Second edition) HSE Books 2000 ISBN 978 0 7176 2488 1

Workplace health, safety and welfare. Workplace (Health, Safety and Welfare) Regulations 1992. Approved Code of Practice L24 HSE Books 1992 ISBN 978 0 7176 0413 5

Safety of pressure systems. Pressure Systems Safety Regulations 2000. Approved Code of Practice L122 HSE Books 2000 ISBN 978 0 7176 1767 8

Safe use of work equipment. Provision and Use of Work Equipment Regulations 1998. Approved Code of Practice and guidance L22 (Third edition) HSE Books 2008 ISBN 978 0 7176 6295 1

Design of plant, equipment and workplaces. Dangerous Substances and Explosive Atmospheres Regulations 2002. Approved Code of Practice and guidance L134 HSE Books 2003 ISBN 978 0 7176 2199 6

Storage of dangerous substances. Dangerous Substances and Explosive Atmospheres Regulations 2002. Approved Code of Practice and guidance L135 HSE Books 2003 ISBN 978 0 7176 2200 9

Control and mitigation measures. Dangerous Substances and Explosive Atmospheres Regulations 2002. Approved Code of Practice and guidance L136 HSE Books 2003 ISBN 978 0 7176 2201 6

Safe maintenance, repair and cleaning procedures. Dangerous Substances and Explosive Atmospheres Regulations 2002. Approved Code of Practice and guidance L137 HSE Books 2003 ISBN 978 0 7176 2202 3

Dangerous Substances and Explosive Atmospheres. Dangerous Substances and Explosive Atmospheres Regulations 2002. Approved Code of Practice and guidance L138 HSE Books 2003 ISBN 978 0 7176 2203 0

HSE guidance/forms

HSE publications are available for free download at www.hse.gov.uk

A guide to the Gas Safety (Management) Regulations 1996. Guidance on Regulations L80 HSE Books 1996 ISBN 978 0 7176 1159 1

Safety signs and signals. The Health and Safety (Safety Signs and Signals) Regulations 1996. Guidance on Regulations L64 (Second edition) HSE Books 2009 ISBN 978 0 7176 6359 0

A guide to the Reporting of Injuries, Diseases and Dangerous Occurrences Regulations 1995 L73 (Third edition) HSE Books 2008 ISBN 978 0 7176 6290 6

A guide to the Pipelines Safety Regulations 1996. Guidance on Regulations L82 HSE Books 1996 ISBN 978 0 7176 1182 9

Form F2508/2508A *Report of an injury, dangerous occurrence or case of disease under* RIDDOR 1995 HSE Books 1996 ISBN 978 0 7176 1078 5

Form 2508G1 *Report of flammable gas incidents* HSE Books 1999 ISBN 978 0 7176 2499 7

Form 2508G2 *Report of dangerous gas fittings* HSE Books 1999 ISBN 978 0 7176 2506 2

You can also report an incident online at www.hse.gov.uk/riddor/online.htm

UKLPG Codes of Practice and guidance

Code 1 *Bulk LPG storage at fixed installations.*
Part 1: *Design, installation and operation of vessels located above ground* (January 2009)
Part 2: *Small bulk installations for domestic purposes* (January 2000)
Part 3: *Examination and inspection* (September 2006)
Part 4: *Buried/mounded LPG storage vessels* (February 2008)

Code 7 *Storage of full and empty LPG cylinders and cartridges* (March 2004)

Code 17 *Purging LPG vessels and systems* (Agust 2001)

Code 21 *Guidance for safety checks on LPG appliances in caravans* (November 1997)

Code 22 *LPG piping system design and installation* (July 2002)

Code 24 *Use of LPG cylinders.*
Part 1: *The use of LPG cylinders at residential and similar premises* (July 2006)
Part 3: *The use of LPG in mobile catering vehicles and similar commercial vehicles* (May 2000)
Part 4: *The use of LPG for catering and outdoor functions* (March 1999)
Part 5: *The storage and use of LPG on construction sites* (May 2000)
Part 6: *The use of propane in cylinders at commercial and industrial premises* (May 2000)

These publications are available from UKLPG, www.uklpg.org

Institution of Gas Engineers and Managers (IGEM) technical publications

IGE/UP/1 Edition 2: *Strength testing, tightness testing and direct purging of industrial and commercial gas installations*

IGE/UP/1A Edition 2: *Strength testing, tightness testing and direct purging of small, low pressure industrial and commercial Natural Gas installations*

IGE/UP/1B Edition 2: *Tightness testing and direct purging of small Natural Gas installations*

IGE/UP/2 Edition 2: *Installation pipework on industrial and commercial premises*

IGE/UP/3 Edition 2: *Gas fuelled spark ignition and dual fuel engines*

IGE/UP/4 Edition 3: *Commissioning of gas fired plant on industrial and commercial premises*

IGE/UP/6 Edition 2: *Application of compressors to Natural Gas fuel systems*

IGE/UP/7 Edition 2: *Gas installations in timber framed and light steel framed buildings*

IGE/UP/9 Edition 2: *Application of Natural Gas and fuel oil systems to gas turbines and supplementary and auxiliary fired burners*

IGE/UP/10 Edition 3: *Installation of flued gas appliances in industrial and commercial premises*

IGE/UP/11: *Gas installations in educational establishments*

IGE/UP/12: *Application of burners and controls to gas fired process plant*

IGE/GM/4 Edition 2: 2008 *Flow metering practices inlet pressure exceeding 38 bar and not exceeding 100 bar*

IGE/GM/5 Edition 3: *Selection, installation and use of electronic gas meter volume conversion systems*

IGE/GM/6 *Specification for low pressure diaphragm and rotary displacement meter installations with badged meter capacities exceeding 6 m^3/h (212 ft^3/h) but not exceeding 1076 m^3/h (38 000 ft^3/h)*

IGE/GM/7A: *Electrical connections for gas metering equipment*

IGE/GM/7B: *Hazardous area classification for gas metering equipment*

IGE/GM/8 - Part 1 *Non-domestic meter installations. Flow rate exceeding 6 m^3/h-1 and inlet pressure not exceeding 38 bar. Design*

IGE/GM/8 - Part 2 *Locations, housings and compounds*

IGE/GM/8 - Part 3 *Installation and commissioning*

IGE/GM/8 - Part 4 *Operation and maintenance*

IGE/GM/8 – Part 5 *Notices and labels*

IGE/SR/20: Edition 2 *Dealing with reported gas escapes*

IGE/SR/23 *Venting of Natural Gas*

IGE/SR/24 *Risk Assessment Techniques*

IGE/SR/25 *Hazardous area classification of Natural Gas installations* (Download amendments (2005) at www.igem.org.uk)

IGEM Standards, PO Box 2584, Uttoxeter ST14 9AB, Tel: 01889 561431
www.igem.org.uk

Building Regulations

To look at relevant Building Regulations go to www.planningportal.co.uk

The Stationery Office publications are available from The Stationery Office, PO Box 29, Norwich NR3 1GN Tel: 0870 600 5522 Fax: 0870 600 5533 email: customer.services@tso.co.uk Website: www.tso.co.uk (They are also available from bookshops.) Statutory Instruments can be viewed free of charge at www.opsi.gov.uk.

Sources of other relevant information

General advice on gas safety issues

Free advice may be obtained by ringing the HSE Gas Safety Advice Line on 0800 300 363 or from the Gas Safe Register on 0800 408 5500 (www.gassaferegister.co.uk).

National Accredited Certification Scheme for gas fitting operatives

Information, including on assessment standards, accredited certification bodies and training providers is available from Energy and Utility Skills, Friars Gate, 1011 Stratford Road, Shirley, Solihull B90 4BN Tel: 0845 077 9922; Fax: 0845 077 9933; Web: www.euskills.co.uk.

Safety scheme for boats on inland waterways

Details of the British Waterways/Environment Agency Boat Safety Scheme may be obtained from the Boat Safety Scheme, 64 Clarendon Road, Watford, Herts WD17 1DA, Tel: 01923 201278 Fax: 01923 201420. In the case of inland waterways not covered by this scheme, advice on safety requirements should be sought from the navigation authority concerned.

Appendix 5

Diagrams of typical installations

Guidance

1   These simplified installation diagrams are only intended for use as an aid to identify and indicate the relative positions of components described in the Regulations, ACOP and guidance.

2   It must be stressed that the diagrams are only general illustrations of typical arrangements and variations may therefore occur in specific circumstances. For instance, in certain cases (eg diagrams c(ii), (d) and (f)) the 'common' or 'remote' valve shown as the first emergency control downstream of the distribution main will not in fact be an emergency control, where intended for use by the gas transporter and/or emergency services rather than gas consumers. In such cases, a valve or valves downstream (eg within individual dwellings) will act as the first emergency control and define the boundary between the service pipe and installation pipework.

3   The upstream boundary of the service pipe (ie with the distribution main) in diagrams (a)–(f) is not shown.

(a) Outside meter installation

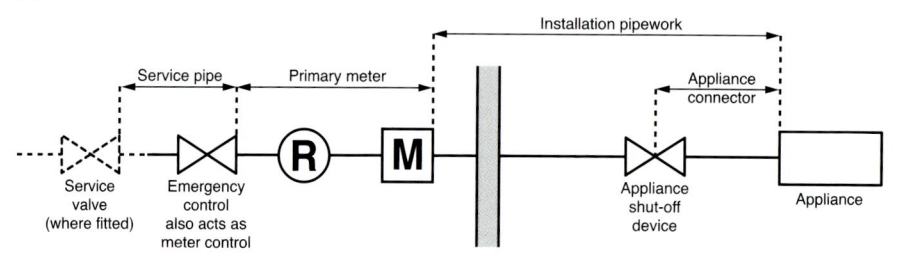

(b) Inside meter installation

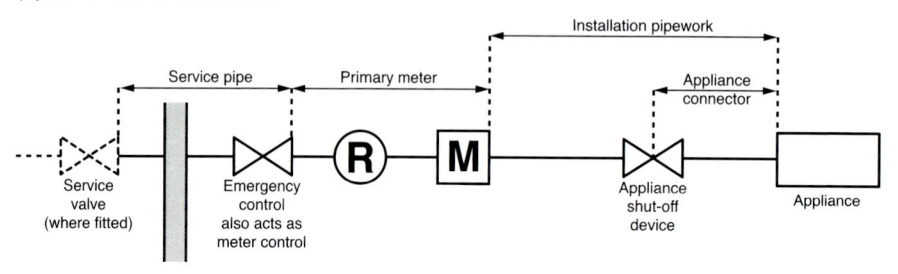

(c)(i) Multi-occupancy installation – external riser

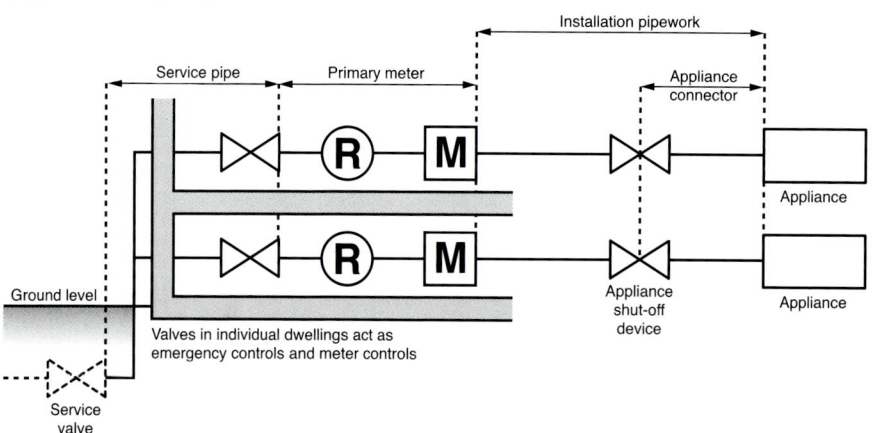

Safety in the installation and use of gas systems and appliances

(c)(ii) Multi-occupancy installation - internal riser

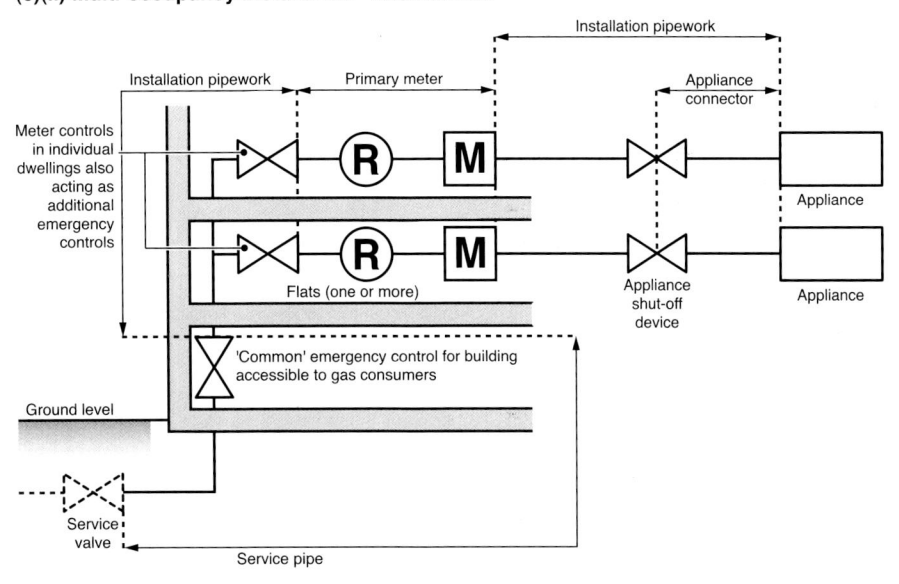

(d) Multi-occupancy installation (remote meters)

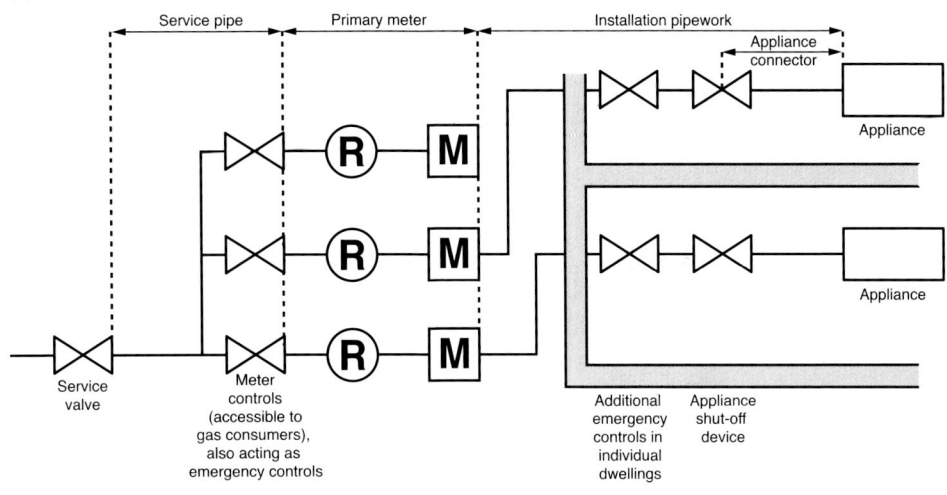

(e) Meter with bypass, eg industrial/commercial

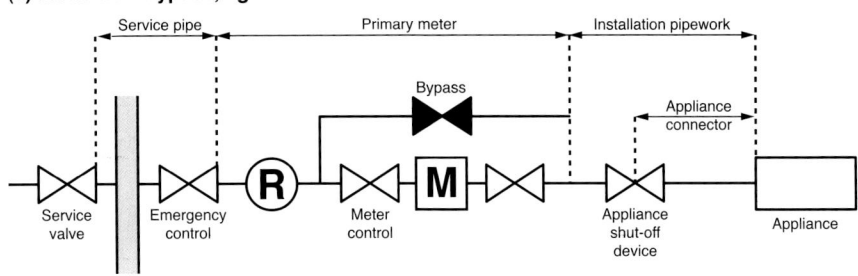

(f) Meter remote from premises, eg meter houses

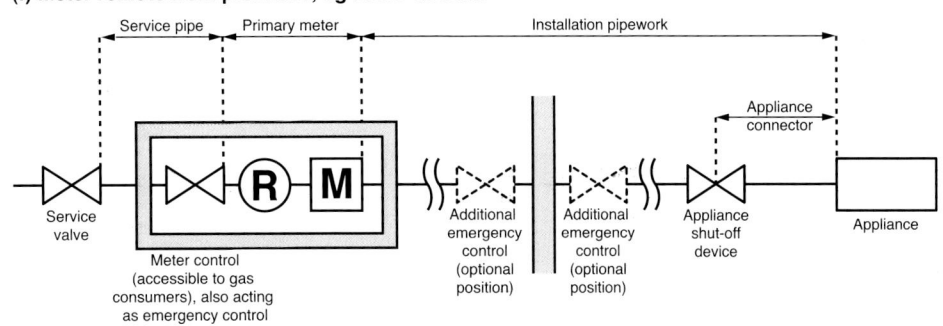

Appendix 5

Guidance

(g)(i) LPG systems – cylinder installation

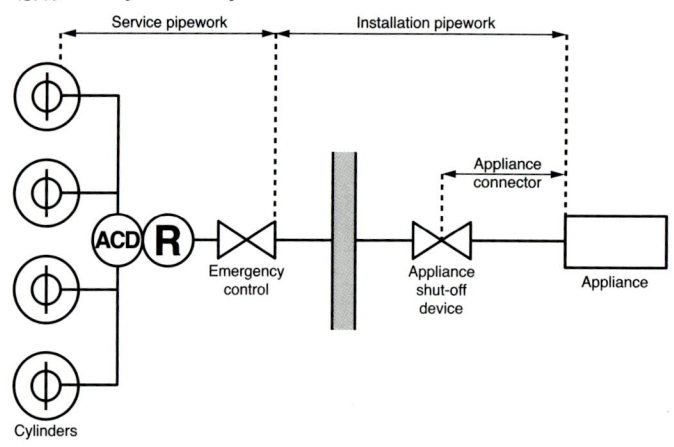

Service pipework | Installation pipework

Cylinders — ACD — R — Emergency control — [wall] — Appliance shut-off device — Appliance connector — Appliance

(g)(ii) LPG systems – single bulk tank installation

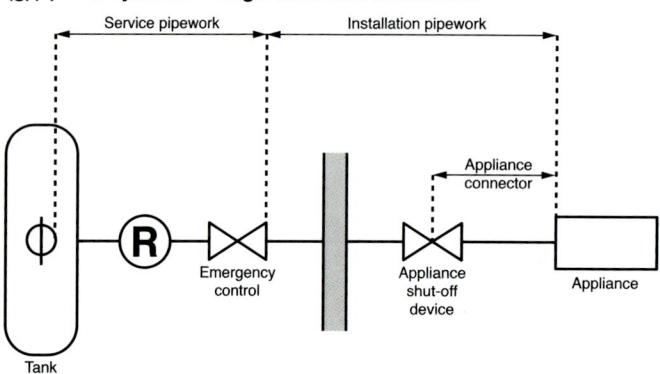

Service pipework | Installation pipework

Tank — R — Emergency control — [wall] — Appliance shut-off device — Appliance connector — Appliance

(g)(iii) LPG systems – single bulk tank installation (multi-residence)

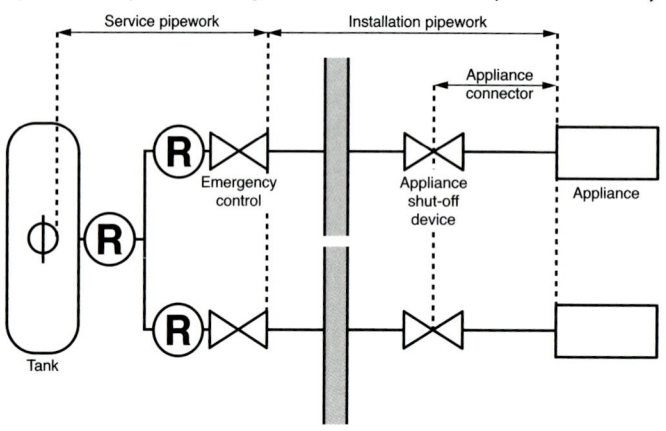

Service pipework | Installation pipework

Tank — R — R — Emergency control — [wall] — Appliance shut-off device — Appliance connector — Appliance
     — R — Emergency control — [wall] — Appliance shut-off device — Appliance

Key:

- **R** Regulator
- **M** Meter
- ⋈ Gas emergency control - situated as near as is reasonably practical to the point where the pipe supplying gas enters the premises or building (see also paragraph 2 of this appendix)
- ⏀ Vapour valve on the storage vessel
- **ACD** Automatic change-over device

Appendix 5

Further information

HSE priced and free publications can be viewed online or ordered from www.hse.gov.uk or contact HSE Books, PO Box 1999, Sudbury, Suffolk CO10 2WA Tel: 01787 881165 Fax: 01787 313995. HSE priced publications are also available from bookshops.

For information about health and safety, or to report inconsistencies or inaccuracies in this guidance, ring HSE's Infoline Tel: 0845 345 0055 Fax: 0845 408 9566 Textphone: 0845 408 9577
email: hse.infoline@connaught.plc.uk or write to HSE Information Services, Caerphilly Business Park, Caerphilly CF83 3GG.

An online version of this can be found online at: www.hse.gov.uk/pubns/books/l56.htm

British Standards can be obtained in PDF or hard copy formats from BSI: http://shop.bsigroup.com or by contacting BSI Customer Services for hard copies only Tel: 020 8996 9001 email: cservices@bsigroup.com.

Safety in the installation and use of gas systems and appliances